THE LOST VALLEY

J. M. WALSH

The Lost Valley

J. M. Walsh

PO Box 2211
Fairfield, IA 52556
www.1stworldlibrary.com
First Edition

LCCN: 2006935238

Softcover ISBN: 1-4218-2491-4
Hardcover ISBN: 1-4218-2391-8
eBook ISBN: 1-4218-2591-0

1st World Library Literary Society

Giving Back to the World

"If you want to work on the core problem, it's early school literacy."

- James Barksdale, former CEO of Netscape

"No skill is more crucial to the future of a child, or to a democratic and prosperous society, than literacy."

- Los Angeles Times

Literacy... means far more than learning how to read and write... The aim is to transmit... knowledge and promote social participation."

- UNESCO

"Literacy is not a luxury, it is a right and a responsibility. If our world is to meet the challenges of the twenty-first century we must harness the energy and creativity of all our citizens."

- President Bill Clinton

"Parents should be encouraged to read to their children, and teachers should be equipped with all available techniques for teaching literacy, so the varying needs and capacities of individual kids can be taken into account."

- Hugh Mackay

CONTENTS

PART I - THE POSTHUMOUS PUZZLE OF MR. BRYCE

PART II - THE ADVENTURES OF MR. ABEL CUMSHAW

PART III - THE FINDING OF THE LOST VALLEY

PART I

THE POSTHUMOUS PUZZLE OF MR. BRYCE

CHAPTER I

THE ADVENTURE ON THE SANDS

I came upon the place quite unexpectedly. Centuries of wind and wave had carved a little nook out of the foot of the cliff and fashioned it so cunningly that I did not see it until I was right on top of it. After the warmth of the open beach and the glare of the white road I had recently travelled its shade looked so inviting that I limped in under the overhang of the cliff and dropped joyfully on to the cool patch of sand. It was the first moment of contentment I had known for many weary months, and, needless to say, I set myself out to make the most of it. I was absolutely sick of tramping about. My left boot had burst and, by the feel of it, there wasn't too much left of my right sole. I had been crawling along the road since daylight - and for many days before for that matter - searching for a job that failed to materialise.

Jobs, it appeared, were just about as scarce as cool spots in Hades. They had been very kind to me at the last farmhouse. The good lady had given me an excellent breakfast and an extra glass of milk, had loaded my bedraggled pockets with food and had finally put me on the road to the sea. Work, she said, they could not give me. They had put off two men the previous day. I might find something to do in the next town.

She did tell me what it was called, but my thoughts were on my own poor prospects and I didn't quite catch what she said. On the principle that a rose by any other name would still have its thorns, I didn't ask her to repeat it. I just said, "Thank you, ma'am," in my best tramp manner and set off down the road to the sea. On the way my left boot burst and a pebble worked in through the opening and set me limping. To make matters worse the day was perhaps the hottest of all that memorable summer, and the glare from the white grit of the road played the devil with my eyes. I was very pleased when at length I reached the low sand dunes and dropped between them on to the wet sand of the beach. I walked along this aimlessly for a mile or so until the big hump of the bluff rose up over me. Then, as I have already related, I came across that heaven-sent cave and threw my weary length on its damp flooring of sand, determined to snatch as much peace and repose as I could before I continued my search for work.

I can't say for the life of me how long it was before I first sat up and took notice of the fat little man. He was bobbing up and down in the surf for all the world like some ungainly porpoise, and every time he moved he shot sunlit streams of water off his gross body. I've seen fat men in my time, but this one was just about the limit. He was all up and down and then across. I know that doesn't quite explain what he looked like, but it's about the only way I can describe him. He was short and tubby; if he had been any shorter he would have been a human Humpty-Dumpty. He was so obviously enjoying himself and getting the best out of his gambols in the water that my heart went out to him. He was ducking and splashing about, rolling and wallowing in a way that reminded me of a hippopotamus I had once shot at - and missed - in happier if not more spacious days spent on the lower Nile. "The Hippo" I christened him, and then chuckled to myself at the singular appropriateness of the name.

Even his bathing dress seemed designed expressly to add to his rotundity. It was one of those queer garments bearing a faint resemblance to a convict's uniform, and the wide stripes of it went round and round his figure like hoops on a barrel. It was so funny that I chuckled again and forgot all about my burning feet and my burst boot.

Presently he stopped his antics and looked over my way. He gave one glance at me, and then started to run inshore with short, jumpy little steps. Something seemed to have struck him all of a sudden, and I was just beginning to wonder what the deuce it could be when, out of the corner of my eyes, I caught sight of a pile of neatly folded clothes thrust into the cleft of the rock a little above my head. I began to understand then. I looked more disreputable than I really was; my suit was in the last stages of ruinous decay, while his brand-new clothes just above me would have been a gift from the gods to a man with less conscience and more figure than I possessed. He evidently presumed on the strength of my proximity that I had evil designs on his clothes, but he needn't have troubled himself. If I could judge anything from his own figure I would have been completely lost in them. I didn't like to confirm his suspicions by running away now that I found I was observed, so I just sat there and waited for him. There was a piece of something that looked very like driftwood protruding from the sand close to me, and I kicked idly at it as he came pounding up the beach. It was set loosely in the sand, and a more accurate kick than usual knocked it out of its resting-place. Something queer about it caught my eye, and I bent over to pick it up.

"Whatever else it is, it isn't driftwood," I said to myself. "I'll bet - ," and then I stopped short, for I remembered that my sole worldly wealth at the moment consisted of exactly three pennies. All the same I was right about it. Driftwood doesn't get the dry rot, nor does it come ashore covered with rich black loam.

"Somebody's planted it here," was my next thought, and my mind strayed to the panting bulk of a man who was thundering down on top of me.

"It's his, I suppose," I said, and looked up at him. At that precise instant he tripped and fell full length on the sand. I've seen a good many lucky escapes in my day - a man who has travelled the out-of-the-way places of the world from the Yukon and the White Nile down to the headwaters of the Fly River in the snow-mountains of Dutch New Guinea does see a bit of life - but the way that fat chap upset himself into the sand was the most wonderful piece of good fortune I ever came across. He must have missed death by a fraction of an inch. I saw him fall, heard the shot ring out and watched the sand spurt up all in the one crowded second. The next moment I was running towards him, my hand moving instinctively to my empty pistol-pocket. But my mind readjusted itself in a flash, and I recollected that I wasn't dodging cannibals in the upper reaches of the Mambare, but was living in a civilised country where a man who carries a revolver, and gets caught at it, is fined more money than I'd seen in the last twelve months.

The other chap seemed to divine instinctively that I was a friend, for he yelled at me even while he was hauling himself up from the sand.

"There's one in my pocket," he shouted and gesticulated back towards his clothes.

I didn't waste a moment, but sped over the intervening yards like a man possessed. As luck would have it his coat was the first thing I grabbed, and the weight of it told me at once in which pocket to look. I plunged my hand in and drew out the sweetest little automatic it has ever been my lot to handle. As a rule I prefer a Colt - in my experience it never jams - but I rather fancied my present weapon would do all that was required, so I slipped back the safety catch with my thumb and whirled round on my heel to face whatever was coming.

The overture was already over and the invisible marksman had settled down to steady firing. The fat man was now almost on top of me, and I saw instantly that that brought me right into the line of fire. It takes a long time in the telling, but, as I figured it out afterwards, from the instant the first shot missed the old chap down to the moment I pulled the trigger, more than half a minute could not have elapsed.

There was only one place in sight where a man could take cover, and that was a bunch of rocks just a little to the left of my position. I let off a fancy shot in that direction, and a second later the reply rang out. The cliff overhead shed a shower of dust on top of the pair of us, and the fat man crouched into the corner. I knew now where my man was, so I waited until he exposed himself, as I saw he must do when he fired again.

"Gimme the gun!" the fat man demanded in the interval.

"Shut up!" I said, without turning my head. "I'm a better shot than you, I reckon, and, anyway, it's just as much my funeral now as yours. He's had a shot at me, and that's a thing I don't forgive in a hurry."

"Well, of all the - ," I heard him say, and then the rest of his remark was drowned in the report of my weapon. I had spotted a white wrist back of a gleam of polished metal and, taking a sporting chance, I let drive. The other man's gun dropped to the sand, and a yell told me that I had made no mistake.

"Here's where I come in," I said, and, forgetting the condition of my feet, I sprinted towards the rocks. But the other fellow had decided that the place was getting too hot for him, and he made off along the sand as fast as his legs could carry him. He must have been in excellent trim, for he shot along the heavy track as if he was running on the cinder-path, and I saw before I had gone fifty yards that I hadn't a chance in the world of catching him. Also there were half a dozen black specks of men a mile or so along the beach, and my reason told me that homicide before witnesses wasn't likely to prove a healthy pastime. So I swallowed my pride and, consoling myself with the thought that some day we might meet again, I wheeled about and made back to the nook.

The fat chap had shed his bathing suit and was climbing into his clothes when I arrived. He beamed at me and his whole face crinkled into smiles. I was so afraid that he was going to make a silly speech that I pushed his automatic into his hands and said, "You'd better take this, old man. The other party's in swift retreat and, from the condition of his wrist, I don't fancy you'll receive another billet-doux for some time to come."

"Well, I'm hanged if you're not the coolest chap I've ever laid eyes on," the fat man said admiringly.

"You were nearer being shot," I hinted, "and, if you don't mind me saying so, the sooner you struggle into those clothes of yours and get home to mother, the safer you'll be. I don't object to fighting for you once in a while, but I'll see you further before I make a habit of it."

"Um!" said the fat man, "I'm sorry. I'd hoped to persuade you to take it on permanently."

I thought at first that he was joking, but the way he looked at me showed that he was in deadly earnest. For all his flippancy there was something back of his eyes, a trace of fear that kept peeping out every now and then, that told me he went in danger of his life. I hated to have to refuse him, but I had very good reasons, which I intended to keep to myself, too, for not putting my life into danger too often. So I told him point-blank that if he wanted to hire a bodyguard he'd have to go somewhere else. He wasn't as put out at my reply as I would have expected. Instead he smiled up at me - for all his bulk I towered over him - and there was a touch of gameness in that smile that I rather liked. I couldn't help telling him just what I thought.

"I don't think you want anyone to look after you," I said. "You're as game as they make 'em. I'm pretty used to reading men - I've been in places where my life depended on my ability in that direction - and when I see a fellow smile like you're smiling now, you can take it from me that he's grit all through."

"They'll get me yet," he said with a sigh. "I'm handicapped, you see. I couldn't have sprinted along the beach the way you did. I'd have wheezed. Bellows gone and all that, you know. Too much fat, the doctor says."

"Now, you're just about right there. I don't like to be personal, but now you mention it, you don't seem to have the cut of an athlete."

"And you have," he said, as he insinuated himself into his collar. It was a trifle too small for his neck, and he had to coax it a lot before he got both ends to meet. "You're the type of man I take to instantly, Mr. - ."

He asked me a question with his eyes.

"Well," I said in answer, "if it's any use to you my name's Carstairs, Jimmy Carstairs at that, and I'm an explorer by inclination, gentleman by instinct, and the rolling-stone-that-gathers-no-moss by sheer force of unlovely circumstance. Now you know all that I intend to tell you about myself."

"Um!" he said again. "I had better introduce myself, I suppose. I fancy my card-case's in my coat pocket."

"Don't trouble about a card," I said airily. "I'm not at all fussy. I'm quite willing to take your word for it."

There was a twinkle in his eye, as he replied, that showed he rather appreciated my cheap wit. "Bryce is my name," he said. "You may have heard of it?"

"Can't say I have," I told him, "though I'm pretty certain to see it often if you make a practice of keeping up this guerilla warfare."

It wasn't a nice thing to say, but then I'm never very particular, and if my listeners don't like my remarks they're always welcome to change the subject. When all's said and done there was more in that last jab of mine than met the ear. I wanted very much to know why that sharpshooter should be so extremely anxious to put him out of action. Also he had said "they." There had only been one man behind the rocks, and I could have sworn on a stack of Bibles that there wasn't another human being - with the sole exception of the men a mile or so along the beach - within coo-ee at the time. "You've been there before, my friend," I thought. "This isn't the first time you've flushed a chap with a bit of hardware." From what I could see Bryce hadn't the slightest intention of making me as wise as himself and even the broad hint I gave him didn't seem to move him in the least. He surveyed me steadily for the scrag-end of a minute and then his left eyelid flickered. I knew right enough what that wink meant. It said as plainly as could be that dead men tell no tales and wise men follow their example.

"Now, Mr. Bryce," I said, "I like your company and it pains me to leave you, but I can't stop here for ever. I've got an important engagement at the next town and the sooner I get there the better. Under the circumstances you'll have to excuse me."

He didn't tell me that I was a liar but he went pretty close to it. "The next town's Geelong," he said, "and it's a good fourteen miles away. You might have sprinted along that sand in record time when somebody's life was trembling in the balance, but that doesn't say you can walk fourteen miles on a rotten road on a broiling hot day. And if I wished to be as personal as you are I'd point out that a burst boot doesn't help make the way any easier."

"Bowled out first shot," I told him. "What's your little game?"

"To use your own inimitable phraseology, my little game amounts to this. I've taken a violent fancy to you, Carstairs, and I want to keep you by me. I don't think your luck's been too good lately, but between us I fancy we can mend it. If you want to go into Geelong all you've got to do is wait and come with me. I'm going back shortly, and I'm sure you'd feel much better riding in a motor than travelling on foot."

"Now you mention it," I said, "I can't see why I shouldn't. The only trouble is that some of your excitable friends might see me in your company and include me in the sudden-death stakes."

"Quite likely," Bryce said, with a smile. "I wouldn't be at all surprised if they hid behind a convenient hedge and potted us as we passed. But you needn't come if that's what you're afraid of."

"I'll forgive you this time," I rattled on, "just because you've had such an exciting experience, but don't ever hint anything like that again. I don't know what fear's like."

"Self-praise," said Bryce, "is sometimes the highest form of recommendation. At any rate it shows you've overcome fear, if only the fear of criticism. But to be serious, Carstairs, there's trouble ahead of both of us. My pursuers are getting very game, tackling me in front of a third person, and I've got a funny sort of feeling that they'll catch me napping one of these days. No matter what you say or do, you can't alter the fact that you've identified yourself with me, and that means that you're running just the same amount of danger that I am. You don't look too prosperous yourself. What about joining forces with me and sharing the plunder? Of course I can make it worth your while."

"Plunder," I said. "What do you mean! Are you running up against the law?"

"If it's any relief to you to know it, I'm not. I rather fancy I've got the law on my side."

"I was merely enquiring what inducements you had to offer. What do you call 'making it worth my while?'"

When I turned down his first tentative offer I had quite made up my mind that he wanted to engage me as a sort of super-butler with sudden death included amongst the risks of service, and I had no intention of mixing up in other people's quarrels on such terms. When I questioned him directly about it I got a pleasant surprise.

"Well, my idea of making it worth your while is something like L100 for three months. That's about as long as I'll require you. After that you can 'go to hell or to Connaught,' whichever you prefer."

"That's nice hearing," I told him. "And, I suppose, any time I take an extra risk I get something *pour boire*?"

He nodded cheerfully.

"That's my offer, Carstairs," he said. "What do you say to it?"

"It's so damned alluring," I answered, "that I'm frightened to look at it too close. I don't mind admitting that I'm about as hard up as I can be. As a matter of fact I've not the least idea where I'm going to get my next meal. All of which makes your offer doubly inviting. But I don't want to jump at it in hot blood. I want time to think it over. I want to stand off and wave my hat at it and say, 'Scat, you brute!' and see if it'll shoo off. I'm frightened that it's not real, and that I'll take it on and then wake up. Will you give me time to wake up?"

"If you'll drive in with me the two of us can dine together," Bryce suggested. "That ought to give you time to wake up."

"I can't ask anything fairer than that," I agreed. "When do we start?"

"No time like the present. I've got the car paddocked down near the reserve. It's only a matter of walking around the bluff. Come on."

I went along with him without comment, though I noticed that the last thing he did was to bend down and pick up the piece of wood which had so excited my curiosity earlier in the proceedings. It was small enough to slip into his pocket, and this he did without a word either of apology or explanation.

"It's a mighty innocent piece of wood," I thought, "but I'll bet all Australia to an albatross that it's mixed up in the plot."

As we moved around the foot of the bluff I couldn't help turning the situation over in my mind. Half an hour before I had been a wanderer on the face of the earth, a man with no special abilities and no outstanding vices. In that short space of time I had saved one man's life, nearly taken that of another, and seemed in a fair way to make money out of my twin attributes of steady nerves and good shooting. I was still thinking in this strain when we rounded the bluff and commenced to crawl across the intervening stretch of spinifex grass. I say "crawl" advisedly. Bryce was far too heavy to do more than lumber along and my feet were steadily getting worse. The spinifex grew knee-high and its roots extended in all directions. They were hard, knobby things that protruded through the loose sand, and every time I took my attention off the ground for an instant I stubbed my toe against one or the other of them. Bryce panted and puffed and wheezed and seemed more like an hippopotamus than ever. Whatever might be the gain as far as decency was concerned, his clothes, from a spectacular point of view, made him look worse than ever. His collar was tight, and that made his face the color of a scraped carrot, and his coat and trousers clung to him in the most unexpected places - just where they shouldn't.

To make a long story short, we came at last to the edge of the spinifex, and thence dropped steadily down into the hollow that contained the reserve. I picked out Bryce's car right off. It was painted a battleship grey, and if cars can have a personality, this had such another as its owner. It wasn't slim - there was nothing of the racer about it. It was squatly built and had just the same heavy and humorous look as Bryce himself.

It stood out from the other cars like a hunch-back amongst a line of athletes.

"That's my car," said Bryce proudly. "She's not much to look at, but she's just the sweetest runner you've seen."

I nodded. I was quite open to conviction.

CHAPTER II

AN OLD FRIEND

Hitherto events had moved so swiftly that I hadn't had time to look calmly at the situation, but once we settled down in the car and Barwon Heads dropped into the dust behind us, I began to think rather seriously. It was perfectly obvious, even to a more clouded intelligence than mine, that there was something mysterious, if not shady, about my prospective employer. Despite his assurance that the law was on his side, I had grave doubts. If everything was perfectly square and above board why the deuce didn't he report the affair to the police and give them the task of looking after him, instead of hiring me at an exorbitant wage? He seemed anxious to fight shy of publicity in any shape or form and, though he had been very cordial, even familiar with me, his very apparent frankness and joviality had awakened my suspicions. There was something fishy going on, and that something, whatever it was, centred round the piece of wood that I had so casually kicked out of the sand. It struck me all of a heap that nothing had really begun to happen until I had unearthed it. As soon as Bryce had seen where I was sitting, he had started to run inshore, the other man had stationed himself behind the rocks, the curtain had been rung up and the play had begun. Now the question was what part did the piece of wood play in the game? Bryce, I felt sure, could clear the mystery up with a word, but I was certain that it would be long before he would say that word.

The car was all and more than he had said. It had speed, it

wascomfortable, and its mechanism was far less complicated than any I had yet seen. We ate up distance in fine style. Bryce seemed to have no nerves at all, for more than once he tore round corners on two wheels while I clung to the side of the car and swore at him. He grinned cheerfully over his shoulder at me and asked me if I were nervous.

I laughed back at him with as much *sang-froid* as I could muster. I had no objection to risking my life once in a while when there was good pay at the end of it, but I couldn't see the sense of tempting Providence just for the sheer fun of the thing. Of course, if we did spill, it would be all right with Bryce - he was so fat that he'd just bounce - but I was slimmer, and I knew from experience that I had very brittle bones. Once in the Solomons, when a wild boar charged me, I lay for weeks in a trader's hut waiting for an obdurate fracture to knit up again. Some idea of the furious pace at which Bryce pushed the car along can be guessed from the fact that we did the fourteen miles in something over twenty minutes. It had been quite half-past eleven when we left the Heads, and the clock in the car wanted a few minutes to twelve when we sailed over the bridge and up Moorabool-street. We cleared a stationary tram by inches, twisted in an S curve to avoid a farmer's waggon and then, with a heart-rending grind, Bryce threw over his clutch and slowed down to a snail-like crawl of ten miles an hour.

"This asphalt paving makes a great motor track," Bryce said to me, "but there's speed-laws in existence here. That's the trouble of it. When a man has a nice track he's interfered with, and when there isn't anyone to meddle with him it's ten to one that he's crawling over something like a corduroy road."

"Corduroy!" I said, and sat up and looked at him. I knew what he meant. Any man who has ever travelled the heart-breaking log-roads of the interior New Guinea goldfields does not need to be told what 'corduroy' is. It is an ever-present memory, an astonishment and a nightmare. Bryce did not speak from hearsay - the note in his voice told me that - but was talking from experience garnered at great cost, both of money and energy.

"Corduroy," he repeated after me. "Doesn't that sound familiar to you, Carstairs?"

"It does," I said with emphasis. "But how the deuce - ?" And then I stopped dead. Bryce? Bryce? What was familiar about that name? Bryce and New Guinea and - . I had it. And Walter Carstairs.

"Ever heard of Walter Carstairs?" I questioned.

"The minute I heard your name I knew you," Bryce said. "Ever heard of Walter Carstairs? Why, he was the best friend I ever had. He saved my life in the early days of the Woodlarks."

"According to the Dad," I said, looking him straight in the face, "it was the other way about."

He laughed happily. "Jimmy, I'm losing my memory if that's so. But whatever happened to him? I lost sight of him the last ten years or so."

"You would," I answered. "He stuck to the Islands. He had a life's work planned out, but he got cut-off in the Solomons before he had reached finality. I carried it on after that, came all the way from the Klondyke to take it up. I got through but it took every penny I had, and that's why this morning when I came across you I only had a boot and a half to my feet."

"Well, well," he said kindly, "that's all changed now."

"I don't know so much about it," I told him. "You might have been the best friend the Dad ever had, but that doesn't say you're going to keep me. What I get I work for. I'll take charity from no man living."

Again he laughed, and his fat face crinkled up into little rolls of flesh until he looked as if he had double chins all the way up to his eyes. I knew now why he had been so familiar with me earlier in the day. He was a sunny-natured old chap always, even in the hard, toilsome New Guinea days, and I suppose his heart went out to me as the son of an old comrade in arms, doubly so - perhaps because I had saved his life. On the whole I rather wished I hadn't. It complicated matters so. It made me feel bound to give him a hand, whether his enterprise was shady or not.

If he had turned to me then and said, "I suppose I can count on you all right?" I would have been torn between duty and inclination. He did nothing of the sort. He made no reference to his offer of service, in fact he seemed to have completely forgotten it, and I thought it just as well to say nothing. The way he forebore from seizing a perfectly obvious advantage sent him up fifty per cent. in my estimation, and by the time we had reached the heart of the city I was quite willing to do anything he asked me.

"I'll park the car," he said, "and then we'll go off and have some dinner."

"Will we?" I said and eyed my tattered raiment ruefully. "I don't fancy I'm dressed for dinner."

"Um!" he said. "You're not. I'd quite overlooked that. That bars a public dinner. I don't fancy you'll be able to make much of one if you come down to my place. The cook's away. I didn't expect to be back so soon."

"Cook or no cook," I told him, "if you've got anything eatable in the house I'll guarantee to turn it up right. Give me the run of the kitchen and put me next to the meat-safe, and you'll see wonders. I don't know how you feel, but I'm so hungry that I'd make a meal off a pair of kid boots."

"In that case, Carstairs, I think I'd better take you home and see what sort of a culinary expert you are."

With that he twisted the car about and headed out for the eastern suburbs. The place was unfamiliar to me at the time - I hadn't the faintest idea of the street the man lived in - and in the face of what happened later I made no enquiries. As a matter of fact the rush of events crowded all such petty details out of my mind.

"Can you drive a car?" he asked abruptly.

"I can drive anything but an Andean mule," I told him. "I tried once in the Chilian foot-hills, but after the animal dislocated my shoulder I sort of lost heart."

"I gather from the retiring modesty of your last remark," he smiled, "that you consider yourself an expert as regards all other forms of animal and mechanical traction."

"Quite so. I can always do anything on principle, and I've yet to meet the job that I'm unwilling to tackle!"

He glanced sideways at me. I didn't like the look he gave me. There was too much of appraisement in it, something that was alien to the nature of the man, a sort of cold, calculating shrewdness that made me wonder again if I had not been mistaken in my estimate of him and the extent of his good-nature.

"If you keep on admiring me instead of looking where you're going," I hinted, "you'll end up in a funeral. That motor-bus isn't the sort of thing I'd care to hit."

He twisted the wheel over a fraction and edged out beyond the motor-bus before he replied. "Life is full of thrills," he remarked when at last we reached the comparative security of open space. There was a challenge in his voice that I thought it well to ignore.

"It is," I agreed. "Too much so."

For all the lightness of his speech and the careless ease with which he took unnecessary and avoidable risks I had a feeling that there was deep design under everything he did. Though I couldn't have proved it if I'd been asked, I felt sure that he was trying my nerve. After all there's no better test of that than the crowded traffic of a big city. I've met men who'd cheerfully face a crowd of howling cannibals and yet would develop a very bad case of jumps if asked to cross a street roaring and humming with traffic. Yes, clearly he was testing me.

With a jerk that nearly shot me out of my seat the car pulled up. I stared about me. We had stopped outside a substantial red-tiled house, built in the bungalow fashion. There was a well-kept lawn in front of it, with here and there a trim flower-bed to relieve the monotony of the expanse of grass.

"This is the place," Bryce said. "Just slip down and open that gate, will you?"

He gesticulated towards a six-foot gate at the side of the house. From my position in the car I could see that it opened on a path that ran round the side of the building and almost certainly led to the garage. Accordingly I slipped out on the road, walked up to the gate and found that, by standing on tip-toe, I could just reach the catch at the top. I swung it back, pushed with my weight against the erection and the gate came open.

As I turned to come back to the car I caught sight of a man standing on the opposite corner. He was engaged in lighting a cigarette in the cup of his hands. He seemed to be taking an undue time over it, and that and something that I could not put a name to in his attitude convinced me that he was watching us. His hands were so cupped that they hid his face, but I received an impression, that was almost a certainty, that he was watching Bryce and myself through his fingers. Perhaps my prolonged stare convinced him that I was fully aware of his presence and its meaning. At any rate he twisted on his heel so that his back was turned to us, dropped the match he had been playing with and ostentatiously struck another.

"That gentleman across the road, the one with his back to us, is keeping your house under surveillance," I said to Bryce. "I suppose he's afraid the place'll run away."

"Afraid I'll run away, more likely," Bryce answered. "Evidently he doesn't want to be identified next time we meet. But he needn't worry over that; I wouldn't know him from a bar of soap. We'll leave him alone for the time being, Carstairs, and get this machine in. I don't see any reason why we should let this gentleman delay our dinner."

"No more do I. Let her out."

I stood on the step of the car until it had passed the entrance in safety, then I went back and made the gate fast. But before doing so I just couldn't resist taking a peep at the Roman sentry figure of a man opposite. He was staring straight at the gate - as if that was going to help him in any way - but he was pretty alert. The moment he sighted me he wheeled about and walked off in another direction. But, quick and all as he was, I caught a passing glimpse of him. He had on a blue serge suit, a rather cheap affair as well as I could judge at that distance, and a black felt hat. Somehow I got the impression, though I was too far away to say anything with certainty, that he was not so much sallow as sunburnt. It was more than likely that he had not got a good look at me - in that case he would not know me again, as I flattered myself that there was nothing very distinctive about me. Still, as that marksman behind the rocks must have been taking stock of me for some considerable while, I realised that no definite advantage would accrue from the fact that one of the gang might not be able to identify me. I had no means of ascertaining how many there were in the organisation, and something warned me not to display too much interest in Bryce's presence. When I walked down the path and discovered him backing the car into his garage I made no comment on the situation beyond telling him that the spy had gone temporarily out of business and was at present taking a constitutional down the street.

"All we can do then," Bryce said, "is to let him depart in peace and trust that nothing happens. I wouldn't like any of that bunch to be cut off in the midst of their sins. I've got another end mapped out for them."

"If you figure me in on that, you're mighty mistaken," I said to myself. "I'm the first line of defence, but I'll be hanged if I'm going to carry the war into the enemy's country."

I needn't have been so cocksure about it, for as will shortly be related that was just exactly what I did do.

CHAPTER III

THE STRANGE BEHAVIOUR OF MR. BRYCE

I made an excellent dinner. Bryce's kitchen and the meat-safes attached proved on investigation to contain enough food for a family. First of all I had a wash, and then when I felt a little more presentable, I dug up a frying-pan, asked Bryce if he liked sausages and, being told that he did, thanked Heaven that his tastes were similar to mine and set about cooking them. Now I like my sausages fried nice and crisp, but I have yet to find the lodging-house keeper this side of Gehenna who can fry anything without burning it to a cinder. Though I don't wish to crack up my own work, I'll say this for it - that, if I do like things done any particular way, I can always be sure of pleasing myself if I do the cooking.

I cooked with one eye on the gas-stove and the other on Bryce. I had scarcely set to work before he wandered into the kitchen, found the nail-brush or whatever it was that the cook used for cleaning the pots, washed the black loam off the piece of wood which had so excited my curiosity earlier in the day, and then commenced to scrub it. He used up an inordinate amount of soap and quite a lot of elbow-grease, but when he had finished the wood looked as if it had just been newly cut and trimmed. What took my attention about it was that it was covered from end to end with queer little marks or scratches. These seemed to interest Bryce very much, for he pored over them like an antiquary who has discovered a new kind of hieroglyphics. He got so interested in them that he forgot my presence altogether. Once when I asked him some simple question about the dinner he jumped as if he were shot, colored up and then said, "Oh, I beg your pardon. What did you say?"

I repeated my question and he answered me as if his thoughts were miles away. He was wide-awake enough when I walked over to the kitchen sink on some errand or another to slip the wood into his pocket and face me with a look in his eye that said as plainly as so many words, "You're not going to steal a march on me, my lad. That's for my eyes alone." Only once during the dinner-hour did he say anything that stuck in my memory. On this occasion he turned to me and asked, "Can you use a typewriter?"

"Now, he's going to make a private secretary of me," I thought. "I won't bite." So I looked him straight in the eye and unblushingly answered that I couldn't use one if I tried and hoped he didn't want me to learn, as I was sure I'd only make a mess of it. He seemed rather relieved at that and later in the afternoon, when I heard the "tick-tack" of his machine drifting out from the room in which he had locked himself, I began to wonder just what he had been driving at.

He drifted out to the kitchen later on and asked me to light the fire for him. I did so and he watched it blaze up, and as soon as he was sure that it was well alight he drew that inevitable piece of wood from his pocket, soaked it in kerosene and dropped it into the heart of the fire. I'm hanged if he didn't sit there and watch it until it had burnt into a charred heap of ashes. While he had been attending to it he had left a sheet of typewritten paper down on the table and as he turned to get it it fluttered to the floor. I was the nearer to it so I picked it up and handed it to him. As I did so I caught a glimpse of the characters that covered most of it. I got just the one look at them, but one line I noticed ran somehow like this -

- 31/41/2743 1/23:3; "335 "49 - 5@3 31/41/2534; 3; L

He looked at me queerly as he took the paper. "Have you ever done any timber measurements?" he asked.

"None at all," I answered promptly, and this time I told the truth.

"You wouldn't understand this then," he ran on, indicating the paper, though he was careful not to let me have another look at it.

"I saw some of it," I said off-handedly, as if it were no affair of mine, "and it looked to me like the sort of thing a mathematician would see if he ever got the willies."

"You have a most expressive way of putting things, Carstairs," he said with a smile. There was more than humor in that smile; there was something in it that looked remarkably like relief.

"I can't stand figures of any sort," I volunteered with a fervent hope in my heart that I wasn't over-doing my part. "A sheet of them'd just about give me the D.Ts."

He laughed out loud at that and then, expressing a hope that I would make myself at home, he padded out of the room. It was astonishing how quietly he could walk when he was moving about the house. For all his gross bulk there was something furtive and cat-like about him that told me just how insistent must be the menace of a sudden death. He moved so silently that I never knew he was there until I looked up and saw him. He glided from room to room like some obese ghost. At first it got on my nerves, but pretty soon I settled down to it, and in a day or so got quite used to seeing a silent bulk sliding noiselessly about the house, appearing at all sorts of odd times in all sorts of queer places.

The cook returned about 5 o'clock and seemed rather inclined to take up a high-handed attitude with me, until a few well-chosen words from her master quietened her down a little. She was not slow to show me in other ways that she regarded me as an intruder in the house, and if any one thing about me was more preferable than another it was my room rather than my company. Still as I kept out of her way as much as possible, and as my sole duties consisted in keeping an eye on all strangers that approached the place and in listening for any unaccountable sounds, I came into conflict with her very seldom.

Matters progressed so quietly for the next couple of days that I began to wonder whether I had not fallen into a sinecure after all. Bryce had procured me a decent outfit so that I was now my own man again, ready to argue the right-of-way with all comers. Added to that my feet were well on the mend and my general health was keeping pretty near to the top-notch mark, so I wasn't finding life such a bad thing after all. Bryce worried me but little. At times I went odd messages for him, but all my trips were so arranged that I was never away from the house more than half an hour at a time. The more I thought over the mystery surrounding him the deeper and more inexplicable it became. I knew of whom he was afraid, but I had no more idea of the reason of his fear than I had of the name of the man in the moon. My occupation was more reminiscent of revolutionary South America than of a civilised country, and the thought of it set me wondering whether Bryce had ever lived amongst the volatile Latins on the other side of the Pacific. Come to think of it the one man I had seen closely had been a dark type. It was just barely possible that Bryce had somehow tangled himself in something of the kind. But then that cipher business - I was fully convinced by now that it was some original kind of cryptogram - rather pointed the other way. One of the things I had noticed had been a L sign, and anything dealing with any of the Latin Republics would almost assuredly have been written with a $ sign. Ultimately I came to the conclusion that I had been barking up the wrong tree.

I jotted down the figures that I remembered, but I must have had some of the signs down wrong, for, try as I would, I could make nothing out of them. As a matter of fact the solution was so simple that in the end I only stumbled on it by accident.

Bryce had a bad habit of locking himself in his room for hours at a time, and it occurred to me that such a course wasn't in his own interest any more than mine, so I tackled him about it at the first opportunity.

"Here you are," I said, "paying me for being a mixture of Swiss Guard and watch-dog, but for all the looking-after you get I might as well be miles away. I don't want to be hanging on to your skirts every ten minutes or so, but doesn't it strike you as a reasonable man that you're inviting trouble by locking yourself in so securely?"

"I do that so I won't be disturbed," he urged.

"That's a reason that cuts both ways," I said. "Suppose somebody happened to be in the room when you arrived. Don't you see that he could do all he wanted to do without being disturbed either."

"But you'd hear any uncommon noise," Bryce objected.

"Maybe I would and then maybe I wouldn't. I'm not infallible, you know, and anyway it's quite possible that any visitor you had wouldn't make a row at all. And while I'm on it, wouldn't it be just as well to give me a sketch of the plot? I'm working in the dark as it is, but, if I had some idea of what's at the back of all this, I might be able to look after you better."

"I'm afraid I can't do that," he said slowly, and for the first time since we had met he eyed me with suspicion. There was doubt in his glance, the sort of doubt that a man does not care to see in the eyes of a friend. I saw that I had made a radical mistake in even hinting that I wished to know his secret, and I hastened to make what amends I could.

"I'm sorry," I said, "if you look at it in that way. I was only doing it for your own good. You're paying what's an enormous sum to me, and I'm trying to justify your expenditure. If I know your enemies and all about them, I can certainly plan level and, maybe, occasionally outguess them. That's the only thing I had in mind when I spoke, and if I gave you any other impression I'm sorry I said what I did."

He moved his shoulders in a kind of half-shrug. It was at once a gesture of relief and of dismissal, so without more ado I said, "If there's nothing further you want, I'll make off now. If you want me any time I'll be pottering around the house somewhere."

"Well, there is something I'd like you to do, Jim," he said. "I want half-a-dozen parish maps. Here's the list of them" - he handed me a piece of paper with a few names scribbled on the back - "and here's the money. Go down to the Lands Department and they'll fix you up. Mind that they are large scale maps, the largest they've got. You'd better take the car, and don't be any longer than you can help."

"It's a twenty minutes' run at the outside," I said. "I won't waste any time."

He nodded quite cheerfully to me and went into his room. I heard the key grate in the lock as I walked down the passage and I remember saying to myself, "That habit's going to get him into trouble yet."

I reached the office in record time. They had some trouble in finding the maps I wanted - most of them were of parishes situated around the foot of the Grampians - but in the end they produced some that I fancied would suit my man. My twenty minutes' limit had almost expired and, as it is a matter of pride with me to be punctual, I let the car out a little. That, I suppose, was my undoing, for just as I crossed over the busiest street a motor-lorry swerved out and nearly collided with me. I did some very neat wheel-work, but my new course took me right across to the gutter, and before I had quite realised what had happened I had speared my tyre with a jagged piece of glass. The tyre popped off with a report like that of a small revolver, and the next second I was bumping on the frame. I pulled up as quickly as I could, but the mischief was done and the tyre was just one great rip from end to end. Luckily I carried a spare wheel, but I am an unhandy man at the merely mechanical part of the work, and I took twice as long over it as a professional would have. By the time I was ready to start again my twenty minutes had lengthened into an hour, and somehow the knowledge of that worried me.

I packed my tools anyhow, hopped back into the car and threw over my clutch. The car started with a little jerk that I didn't quite relish, and on looking over the side I saw that the new wheel was wobbling, not very much indeed, but just enough to show me that I had bungled my work. I immediately cut down my speed and proceeded for the rest of the journey at something closely approaching a snail's pace.

"Now," I said to myself, "if this was in a novel I'd say that the lorry cut across my path deliberately. But as this is in real life and the lorry belongs to a firm of respectable grocers it can't be anything else but just my own darned bad luck."

I dismissed the incident at that and turned my attention to my driving. I had no intention of mixing myself up in another such accident if I could possibly avoid it, and now that I had definitely taken service with Bryce I felt I owed it to him to exercise all reasonable care. After my first few spasmodic attempts at resistance I had succumbed rather quickly to his enticing offer. After all, I thought, I wouldn't be putting myself in any greater danger than I had been in for the past four years. I had faced sudden death in many shapes and forms during my sojourn in the strange wild lands about the Line, so much so that, once I had taken into account the money Bryce was giving me, the present adventure rather degenerated into a pleasant little game of hide-and-seek.

I was still turning this over in that portion of my mind which wasn't occupied with the sheerly mechanical side of my work when I reached the house. More from force of habit than from any other cause I cast my eyes along the road, much as if it had been a forest trail that held secrets only a woodsman could read. Plainly marked in the dust of the roadway were the tracks of a vehicle that I instinctively knew to be a cab. It had veered right in towards the kerb, and a moment's study convinced me that it had stopped at Bryce's house. Now that meant that somebody had arrived during my absence, and, as Bryce had said nothing to me about expecting a visitor, I decided that the sooner I entered the house and investigated the better for the safety of all concerned. I drove the car into the garage in record time and darted into the house as if the devil were at my heels. There wasn't a sound to be heard; even the eternal clatter of the typewriter had ceased. With a caution born of experience I tip-toed up the passage, all my senses instinctively on the alert. The door of Bryce's room was still locked and everything, to all outward seeming, was just as I had left it. I don't know what I had expected to find in the passage, but the very apparent quietness of the place sobered me considerably, and I realised abruptly on what a slender foundation I had based my fears. If anything had happened during my absence it was almost certain that I would have found some trace of it in the hall, a rug disarranged, or a mat kicked away from the door. All the odds were on Bryce working quietly behind the locked door. Yet of all the foolish things in the world for me to think of the idea that entered my mind just then was that something that concerned me very intimately was being worked out in the room across the passage.

I made one step forward and then I stopped abruptly. Some one else than Bryce was in the room. Out of the silence came a voice, a woman's voice. It was smooth and well-modulated, and there was the faintest touch of music in it. In some curious way it touched a stray chord in my memory. I knew at once that I had heard it before, but how or where I could no more say than I could fly. Perhaps that was because its full notes were muffled by the door that intervened.

"I'd do anything," the woman said in the quietest tones

imaginable, "anything but that. You don't understand. If you knew all the circumstances, if you knew just how and why we parted you wouldn't ask me. I'm sorry for it all now, more sorry than you could believe, but you can't expect me to take up things just where they left off - as if nothing had happened."

"Bryce's got a little romance tucked away up his sleeve," I thought. "This sort of complicates matters. Wonder who the lady is?"

"My dear girl," came the reply in Bryce's tones, softer and more persuasive than I had ever heard them, "I know more perhaps than you think. I'm doing this out of the fullness of my knowledge in the hope that when I'm gone...."

"Don't!" the woman interrupted sharply. "Don't talk like that!"

"It's one of the things we've got to face," Bryce said gently. "I won't live for ever anyway, and you know as well as I do just what chance I run of having a period put to me ... any time now." The last three words were spoken very slowly and distinctly, as if Bryce wished them to sink into the mind of his companion. "You're the only person in the world that I care a hang about," he continued with a note of indescribable pathos in his voice, "and I'm doing all this for you ... and him."

"But I tell you," the girl said with a little flash of anger, "I tell you I won't have anything to do with him. If you bring him to the house I'll cut him dead."

"And put yourself doubly in the wrong and make it all the harder for everybody," Bryce told her.

There was a dogged note in the girl's voice as she replied. "I know I was wrong, but I just can't do what you want. I can't say more than that."

"I'm sorry you look at things that way," Bryce said. "I had hoped...." I did not catch the nature of his hope, for his voice dropped an octave or so and his sentence ended in whispers.

"Jimmy Carstairs," I said to myself, "you've been eavesdropping and you know it. You mustn't be caught doing those kind of things. Get out of the way as fast as you can," and at that I twisted round on my heel and went back down the hall. I hadn't any desire to be caught listening to conversations that were obviously not intended for me and that anyway weren't of the least interest. So you can be sure that when I did return up the hall I walked fairly heavily and coughed discreetly as soon as I was within hearing distance of Bryce's room.

The key turned in the lock of a sudden and the door was flung wide open. The girl stood in her own light so that the shadows masked her face, but the sun fell full on mine and my features must have been clearly visible to her.

"You!" she said, with a little catch in her voice.

"Shut the door, please," I said, in the most matter-of-fact tones I could muster. "Shut the door and come out here."

I knew her now. God! Could I ever forget her? In a flash my mind flew back through four years - or was it five? - to that evening when she had caused my little world to rock and tremble, and then to fall in pieces at my feet. I had loved her then - I thought I loved her more than anything or anyone in this world - but a dying father's wish had come between us. The poor old Dad had made a life study of the Islands - how monumental a study it was let his three volumes of Solomon Island Ethnology bear witness - yet he died before he had quite completed his notes. Though he had said nothing to me I knew the wish that lay nearest his heart, and I made his dying hour almost the happiest of his life by promising to carry on his work.

I remember the night I came out to tell her. The sky was

streaked with dead gold and cerise and warm-tinted clouds trailed across the heavens like the ends of a scarf streaming from the neck of a hurrying woman. All the world was gay that evening and I whistled as I went. She was waiting at the gate as always she had waited for me. She greeted me with a smile and some bright little remark that I forgot practically the instant it was uttered.

"I want to talk to you," I said; "I want to talk seriously."

She smiled up at me, a trusting little smile as I thought. She had no idea what was coming, but she always gave me my head in the things that do not matter much.

"What is it, Jim?" she asked.

"It's this," I said, and then I told what I had promised.

"But that," she protested, "means burying yourself in New Guinea and the Solomons for four whole years."

"It does," I said. "There is no other way."

I had not been looking at her face - there had been no need, for I was quite convinced that she would see things in a proper light - but now I turned on her. To my surprise there was just the least little touch of annoyance in her face.

"You don't quite relish the idea," I said.

"It's a very foolish idea," she said quite frankly. "I don't know what you could have been thinking of."

"I was thinking of my father," I told her. "I was making his last hour happy, and he died in the knowledge that I would carry his work on to the conclusion he had planned."

"Are you going to see it through?" The abruptness of the question took me aback.

"Of course," I said. "What else could I do?"

"Four years!" she said. "What is to become of me?"

"The time will soon go by," I answered, "and then I'll come back to you and everything will be right."

"You seem to think of everyone but me," she said hotly. "You promised so that your father would die easy, and that's the end of it. If you are going to be bound by such a thing as that you're nothing more than an impractical idealist."

"I passed my word and a Carstairs never breaks a promise."

"You mean that, Jim? You mean that you are going away to ... carry out that absurd promise?"

"It's not absurd," I declared.

"I think it is," she said wilfully. "If you go, you need never come back."

"I am going," I said steadily. "As an honorable man there is no other course open to me. I'm sorry that you look at it this way, but I can't do anything else."

"At last I know how much you think of me," she said with that little touch of anger with which a woman always defends the indefensible. "You never did care for me."

"I do, I do," I protested. "Can't you see it?"

"I can't see anything," she said stubbornly, "except that you'd do this rather than listen to me. It shows all you think of me. Oh, I hate you! I never, never want to see you again!"

"Is that your last word?" I demanded.

"Absolutely my last," she answered firmly.

"Well," I said, "here's my last too. I'm going to carry out my promise, and if a man had spoken to me about it as you have spoken to me to-night I would have pulped his face."

"I really believe you would," she said exasperatingly. "You see, Jim, you were always something of a savage. That, I suppose, is why you are so anxious to go to the Islands ... where the savages are."

That was the very last word she had said to me, for the next moment the gate was banged behind her and shut me out of her life. I was hurt, badly hurt in my self-esteem, but my rising anger, burning hot within me, kept me from feeling as bad as I might have felt. In two months' time I landed at Tulagi on Florida Island, and for the next four years or so the civilised world knew me not. I reached finality, but I spent my fortune and came back to Australia to all intents and purposes a pauper. Four years...! Here she was facing me at last - just as if nothing had ever come between us.

"Yes, it's me," I said ungrammatically. "Why?"

She raised her hand to her throat with a queer little gesture. "I didn't quite expect to see you ... yet," she said.

"It's the unexpected that happens," I remarked. "I've come back at last, though in slightly different circumstances."

"I know, Jim. I've heard."

"He told you," I suggested, and nodded towards the door she had just closed.

"How do you know that?" she asked quickly.

"It is my business to know things," I told her. "I'm a professional caretaker of secrets now."

She looked at me blankly and I saw that he had not told her

everything. It behoved me to play the game warily until I was sure of my ground.

"What are you doing here, Moira?" I asked her point-blank.

"That's a question I could ask you," she countered. "But I am here, not from any desire to meet you - I didn't know you were here - but because he sent for me."

"And why should he send for you?" I persisted.

There was just the faintest flicker of a smile moving about her lips now; she had turned a little and the light was playing on her face.

"For just the simplest reason in the world. He wanted me."

"Why should he want you?" I demanded.

She looked at me a moment as if astonished that I should ask such a question. But there was that in my eyes which told her that my ignorance was anything but assumed.

"You really mean to say you don't know?" she asked incredulously.

"If I did know I wouldn't question you about it," I said shortly. "What is the reason?"

"Well, you see," she answered lightly, with just a slight uplift of her eyebrows - an old theatrical trick that I used to admire in the days gone by - "he happens to be my uncle."

"That puts another complexion on matters," I said half to myself. But her quick ear caught the drift of my remark and she was down on me like the wolf on the fold.

"You're in with him, are you?" she questioned, with that devouring flame I knew so well flaring up in her golden-brown eyes. "You're in with him ... in this?"

In a way I wasn't. As a matter-of-fact I suspected from her last words that she knew more about everything than I did, but I was perfectly sure that she wouldn't believe me if I denied it, so I said instead, "Yes, I am."

"I might have known it," she said with a little shake of her head. I didn't quite follow her logic, but I judged it best to let it pass. One would think from the way she spoke that there was something reprehensible in being mixed up in anything conducted by her venerable relative. I wondered why.

"Yes, you might have known it," I said, falling in with her own humor. "I have a habit of doing things I shouldn't."

I knew she understood my veiled allusion, for I saw her bite her lip and again the lambent flame leaped up in her eyes. But it died as suddenly as it had come, and in another instant the old tantalising smile was playing about the corners of her mouth. In the smoky interminable depths of the Solomon Island jungle I had crushed that smile out of my life, for ever I had thought. I had deliberately erased it from my memory, and at night beside the smudge fire, when my eyes closed for an instant and that beautiful imperious face peeped at me from out of the mazes of recollection, I would open my eyes and stared fixedly at the misshapen headhunters who were my sole companions in that wilderness. "These," I would say, "are the kindred of us both. Their women smile as she smiles, and the men respond to it as I used to respond." And with that thought in my head I would fall asleep and not dream.

"Jim," she said with abrupt irrelevance, "you've changed. You usen't to be like that before. You're different somehow ... cynical, I think."

"That's more than likely," I agreed. "I'm learning to hit back. And now if you'll excuse me," I ran on before she had time to answer, "I'll just drop in with this parcel."

Then without more ado I turned on my heel and knocked at Bryce's door.

CHAPTER IV

THE THIEF IN THE NIGHT

"I've got those maps you wanted," I remarked as Bryce opened the door, "and I hope I haven't kept you waiting too long."

"You haven't," he said with a smile. "As a matter-of-fact I've been otherwise occupied. I've had a visitor."

"A visitor?" I said guardedly, though what on earth there was to guard against was more than I could have said just then. Some cross-grained streak in my nature made me both cantankerous and suspicious, and while the mood was on me I would have contradicted or queried the word of an archangel.

"Yes," Bryce replied. "The lady you met in the passage. I gather that she knows you."

"We knew each other years ago," I said shortly. In a flash the meaning of the conversation I had overheard burst on me. I began to perceive that her presence in the house was due in part at least to me. Well, if he fancied he was going to patch up our old love affair he had undertaken a bigger job than he thought. For two pins I would have told him, had he uttered another word, that there was one matter in which I would brook no man's interference, and that even the ties that bound him to my father were not strong enough to allow him to settle what was nobody's affair but mine. But, with even greater tact than I believed he possessed, he switched the conversation on to quite another subject and talked to me for the better part of half-an-hour about the maps I had brought.

He had the formation of the country and its industries at his fingers' ends, and he spoke like a man who had gained his information at first-hand. I listened attentively, for I guessed in some queer fashion of my own that the maps and that foolish cryptogram, the shooting on the beach and the piece of driftwood were all somehow connected. But either I must have missed some very obvious point or else he picked his words so carefully that he misled me.

I used my eyes for all they were worth, which wasn't much. The typewriter stood on the table in its old position, and the table itself was littered with sheets of typed figures. "More timber measurements," I said to myself. Somehow the sight of those sheets troubled me. They were innocent-looking enough in all conscience, and I couldn't for the life of me understand why they should have this peculiar effect on me. I felt as if a cold gust of wind, the icy breath of Death himself, had passed and touched me in the passing. I flatter myself that I have pretty strong nerves - the Lord knows they've been tested often enough – but there was something in the atmosphere of that room, something in the sight of those littered sheets of paper, that sent a cold shiver through me, that made me want to rush from the place into the golden sunshine out of doors. It was a presentiment, but one that could not be localised. It did not appear to be one that could be shared either, for Bryce still talked on in his own quaint way, apparently unaffected by the strange influence which so troubled me.

At last he rose and proceeded to gather up the disordered papers on the table. I rose too, and with a careless "So long," was making for the door when he stopped me with a question.

"I suppose," he asked, "that you haven't seen anything lately of our inquisitive friends?"

"The Roman sentry and the gentleman with the hardware and

the smashed wrist?" I answered his question with one of mine.

He smiled at my description and the laughter-lines about his mouth creased into a myriad wrinkles. "You have them exactly," he remarked.

"No, I haven't seen them," I said. "They seem to have disappeared into nothingness."

Curiously enough the news, instead of pleasing, seemed to disappoint him. "They evidently mean business," he said in a semi-undertone. It seemed almost as if he was speaking his thoughts out aloud.

He glanced up at me with brooding eyes and brows drawn close together. "We'll hear from them presently," he murmured, "and then the end won't be far away."

"Cheer up," I said hastily, "They've got a long way to go yet, and I don't think they'll find me altogether pleasant to deal with."

"If you knew all about it," he said, and then he hesitated. For just the fraction of a second he trembled on the point of divulging everything, and then his old cautiousness re-asserted itself and the impulse died away.

"That'll be all," he said briskly. "Just keep your eyes and your ears open, Jim, and, as you say, we'll beat them yet."

But I rather fancied from his tone that he meant that last sentence the other way about.

* * * * *

I came awake instantly. The noise that had awakened me still echoed in my ears and, though I could not put a name to it, I could have sworn that it came from the room where Bryce did his typing. It was a very faint noise, not the kind to bring a heavy sleeper instantly awake. But my nerves work like a hair-trigger, and the almost noiseless pad of a cat across the room at night is sufficient to rouse me. What I had heard had been so faint that a less matter-of-fact man might have imagined that he had dreamt it. But I knew better. I don't dream.

The obvious thing was to slip out of bed at once and investigate. I didn't. I knew a trick worth two of that. I sat up and listened. It might be a wandering tabby that had blundered into a piece of furniture; perhaps the window had creaked; it might be any one of half a hundred things. If there was an intruder in the house I felt certain that presently I would hear something more. No man, no matter how careful he be, can move with a complete absence of sound.

Five minutes passed, ten, a quarter of an hour. Nothing happened. And then, just as I was beginning to despair, I heard it again. It was a little plainer this time. Somebody had scraped a chair across the floor and it had creaked slightly.

That was more than enough for me. I slipped out of bed, but I did not hurry. Many a man with the prize almost within his grasp has lost it simply because he has rushed at it with his eyes shut. I didn't dawdle, but I said to myself, "The more haste the less speed, Jim," and accordingly I took my time. Of course if I had fancied that there was one chance in a hundred of the man getting away, I would have been on the spot like a shot, but I guessed from what I had heard that the visitor was in no hurry, and certainly hadn't the faintest suspicion that anyone in the house was aware of his presence. I got my clothes on somehow and took a grip of my long Colt by the barrel end. I didn't want to shoot unless there was no other way out of it, and anyway a revolver-shot kicks up such an infernal racket inside a house and brings on the scene quite a number of people who'd be better at home and in bed.

I slunk down the passage like a shadow, walking as if I were treading on eggs. Very softly I tried the door. To my disgust it was locked. Now the only time Bryce ever locked it was when he was at work inside, so I knew that my man was still within reach. As if to make assurance doubly sure I caught, as I stepped back, the faint gleam of a pencil of light from under the doorway.

The position as I summed it up was this: - The intruder had entered through the door and had quietly locked it behind him. That would have been the first noise I had heard. Then he had hunted about for whatever he wanted and, once it had been found, he had drawn the chair up to the table and settled down to a prolonged study of the matter. That would explain the two sounds. Now as my man had come in through the door he was almost certain to go out the same way and, in the interests of peace and quiet, the proper course to take was to sit down and wait until he decided to come out.

I can't say how long I waited there. It seemed like hours, but of course at the outside it could not have been many minutes. I would dearly have liked to smoke, but I rather fancied that the other man's nose would be sure to scent me out. Also a scrape of a match in a still house at the dead of night sounds like a bomb-explosion. So I just squatted down on my heels and cursed my man under my breath. I was in deadly fear most of the time that he would make a noise of some kind and bring the other inhabitants down about my ears. He was my meat, and I meant to eat him myself.

At length the pencil of light went out. Somebody moved stealthily across the room and the key turned softly in the lock. I balanced the gun in my hand and got ready to swing. It was pitch-dark in the hall and I could not see an inch in front of me, but I had my fingers right up against the jamb of the door and I could feel it opening. The man was breathing with a barely perceptible wheeze and, if I had not been listening for something of the kind, I might have missed it altogether. But it was quite loud enough for me to position the fellow, and the next instant I flopped out of the darkness on to him. He gave a surprised little gasp, a sort of sizzling like the air escaping out of a punctured tyre, and went down on the mat underneath me. I had taken him so completely off his guard that there was no need for me to use my gun. I got one hand on his throat in the most approved style of the garrotte and just pressed. He wriggled a little at first, but I kept up the same even pressure, and presently he went limp. I knew then that he was harmless for the next ten minutes, so I released my hold, slipped my useless Colt into my pocket, and made to stand up. But at that precise moment the electric light in the hall went on, and a silvery voice said, "Hands up, please!"

In the astonishment of the moment I shot my hands heavenwards and turned round to view the new arrival. It was just as I thought. Moira had blundered into my little surprise party, and she was doing her level best to annex all the honors for herself. She was standing with one hand on the light switch and the other held Bryce's automatic. Her face was very pale, and the hand that held the revolver wasn't quite as steady as I could have wished. She blinked a little at me - her eyes seemed blinded by the sudden radiance - and I don't think she recognised me for the moment, so much do one's ordinary clothes make the man.

It was clearly up to me to disillusion her and persuade her either to put down the revolver or hold it in a way less calculated to alarm the peaceful public.

"You'd better put down that infernal thing, Moira," I said calmly, "or you'll be doing someone damage. The mere sight of you makes me nervous, Diana."

There was a studied insult in the last word, but I think somehow she must have missed it in the excitement of the moment, for she lowered her gun and ran towards me.

"Oh, it's you!" she cried surprisedly.

"It's me," I said dourly, and I dropped my hands into a more convenient position. "In fact it's so much me that I'd be obliged if you'd keep quiet for a while and help me look after this gentleman on the floor. I want to examine him, and I don't think I'll be able to do it in comfort if you wake the rest of the family."

"Who is he?" she asked, showing by the subdued note of her voice that she had taken my warning to heart.

"That's more than I can say," I answered. "I discovered him in the room there, and when he came out I promptly sat on him."

"But what did he want?"

"If one can judge anything from his present attitude, he came to study the pattern of the carpet, Moira."

"Be serious, Jim, please."

"I couldn't if I tried," I said, rising to my feet. "It's too much like hard work. But let's look at the captive, Diana."

This time the shot went home, and in a way I was glad. I had four years' arrears to make up yet. It was not a very manly thing to do, I know - it certainly wasn't at all gentlemanly - but it gave me a deuce of a lot of satisfaction, and that's about all I can say in defence. She looked up at me with both hurt and contempt in her eyes, but I was far too engrossed in the business in hand to give her more than passing notice. When I came to think it over in calmer moments I realised that, despite all that had happened, the girl was just as much in love with me as ever she had been.

The fellow was young, at the most he could not have been more than twenty-four or five, and I saw instantly that he was the man I had called the Roman sentry - the chap who had been spying on the house the day Bryce had driven me home from the Heads. The life wasn't crushed out of him by any means; even as I examined him he stirred a little and his eyes opened. They were nice black eyes, the sort that brim over with humor, yet way at the back of them I caught a glimpse of something else. It was a queer mixture of anger and determination, and I saw just sufficient of it to warn me to take no unnecessary risks. Save for that first spasmodic movement he lay perfectly still, those black eyes of his laughing up at me and challenging. Somehow they filled me with a curious sense of unrest, a feeling as if everything that made life safe and secure was slipping away from me. I did not speak a word, however, but gave him back look for look, striving with my eyes to beat down the challenge I read in his. They said as plainly as so many words, "I'm the better man, and I'll beat you yet. Try and see if I don't."

"What are you doing here?" I demanded at length, seeing that one of us must speak, and he seemed the less likely.

"If I told you I was a somnambulist you wouldn't believe me, would you?" he replied.

"I wouldn't," I said tersely.

"I'm not, anyway," he continued, with those infernally self-possessed eyes daring me ... daring me what?

"You've got to explain what you were doing in that room," I threatened. "The sooner you tell me the better it'll be for you."

"It's no use talking like that, my friend," he said. "You won't get a word more out of me than I wish, and while I think of it you'd better call in the police at once and have done with it."

It was the first time that the idea of the police had occurred to me, and, now I came to think of it, it wasn't too acceptable. Without knowing much about it, I surmised that the less Bryce had to do with the police the better he'd be pleased, that is if I could base anything on the way he had behaved that morning on the beach. As it was Moira seemed to have much the same idea as myself, or perhaps she spoke from superior knowledge.

"Don't call the police in, Jim," she said in a quick whisper. "You mustn't do that. It'd be better to let him go."

I shook my head. "I don't want to let him go," I said, "but if you don't want to make an example of him, I don't see what else there is for it. I'll have a word with him first, at any rate, and see what I can make out of him."

"Be careful, Jim," she whispered, all the strain and anger occasioned by my ill-timed insult disappearing in her anxiety for my welfare.

I ignored her admonition, more because I could think of no suitable reply than for any other reason, and addressed myself to the captive.

"Get up," I said. "You and I are going to have a little heart-to-heart talk."

He made no effort to rise, so I leaned over and hauled him up by the collar. By the feel of him he was some forty pounds lighter than I, and I made a mental note of that in case we had a scrimmage on the way. Weight counts a good deal in a rough-and-tumble. I got a good neck-hold on him, and then I turned to Moira. "You'd better get back to bed and forget," I said. "I'll deal with this smart Alec here."

I did not wait to see if she took my advice, but I prodded my captive with my free hand. "Jog along, Eliza," I said. "Straight down the hall, and don't try any monkey tricks."

He went quietly enough; if I had had my wits about me I would have had my suspicions aroused by that same fact. I was flushed with victory, and, what was even more pleasant, I was acting to an impressionable audience. I was sure that Moira could not fail to appreciate the neatness with which I had conducted the whole affair, and, though I kept telling myself that I did not care a hang for her, I hadn't the faintest objection to showing off before her. On the contrary. That, in part at least, was the cause of my undoing.

The hall ended in a big French window that opened out on to the back verandah. It was very seldom used, indeed I had never seen it opened, but there it was with glass all the way to the floor. When I marched my prisoner down the hall I had some vague idea of taking him out on to the verandah and inducing him to tell me what he had come for. But the man had other plans maturing, and when we were just about six or seven feet away from the window he gave a little twist and a wriggle and slipped out of my hands as if he had been an eel. Then, before I had quite recovered sufficiently to make a grab at the empty air, he hurled himself against the window. It was one of those foolhardy things that succeed just because of the sheer, daring recklessness of the man who carries them through. He swept through the glass with a splintering crash that must have been audible for half-a-block away, and then, while the falling pieces still tinkled on the floor, he placed his hand on the verandah rail and vaulted to the ground. I drew my revolver at once - I had been pulling it out of my pocket even as I ran down the all - and took a flying shot at him. But in the hurry of the moment I missed, and I padded out on to the verandah through the splintered window just in time to see him scaling the back fence with the practised ease of the family tabby.

I did not attempt to follow him. I knew the uselessness of such a proceeding. Just for the fraction of a second his hurrying silhouette had shown on the top of the fence, and then it had melted into the surrounding shadows of the dawn with a silence and celerity which, more than anything else, told me how difficult it would be to trace him.

I turned on my heel, only to find that the lights were blazing up in practically every room, and Moira, Bryce and the servants were gathered in a huddled, indecisive group just inside the window. Most of them looked startled. Bryce had been a little shaken, but his self-possession was rapidly returning. Moira, indeed, was the only one who faced me with anything like calmness in her face.

"You'd better all get back to bed," I said, seeing that someone had to take the initiative. "It's nothing very much, nothing to worry you at any rate."

"Yes, you'd better go back," Bryce said, seconding my remarks. "There's nothing doing."

The servants moved away one by one, leaving the three of us together. For quite a minute Bryce eyed the revolver that I still held in my hand, then his glance travelled to the shattered window, and, completing the circle, came to rest on me again.

"Well?" he queried, with intense interest in his voice. I knew what that monosyllable meant. It was a request for a detailed account of the events of that night. Seeing that there was nothing to be gained by withholding anything, I plunged into the tale and related everything just as it had happened.

"So he got away from you?" he remarked when I had finished.

"He did," I said emphatically.

"That's about the best thing he could have done," Bryce ran on. "I don't know what we could have done with him if we had kept him."

"'He who fights and runs away will live to fight another day,'" I reminded him.

"That other day is a matter for the future," he answered. "We'd better see what he took though. Come on."

He turned on his heel and led the way to his study just as the first rays of the rising sun crept up over the distant hills.

CHAPTER V

CIRCUMSTANTIAL EVIDENCE

The room was much as we had left it the evening before. The typed papers had disappeared, but a sheet which I recognised as the one I had picked up from the kitchen floor the day of my arrival lay on the table in full view. Beside it was the clean blotting pad that I had never yet seen used. Bryce took no notice of the sheet of figures, but lifted the pad up, and, drawing a magnifying glass from his pocket, ran his eyes over the rough white surface. Moira and I watched him with unfeigned interest. At last he looked up.

"Just as I thought," he remarked. "Have a look yourself, Jim." He handed both glass and pad to me. I studied the latter for some seconds before I quite dropped to what he meant. Gradually I made out figures impressed on the rough surface. Our midnight visitor had made a copy of that single sheet, had made it hurriedly in pencil, and the impression had gone through on to the receptive softness of the blotting paper. My scrutiny over, I handed the materials to Moira.

"You understand?" Bryce queried, with little laughter-wrinkles about his eyes.

"I do," I said admiringly. "I don't know what the man was after, but he didn't get it. He got a fake instead."

Bryce nodded. "He's up a gum-tree instead of under one," he

said enigmatically.

I made no answer to that, chiefly because it struck me that it was the sort of remark that meant a good deal more than appeared on the surface. I tucked it away in my memory, quite confident that sooner or later the march of events would make it clear to me. As a matter of fact, if I hadn't taken so much notice of that simple sentence, this story would never have been written, for the key to everything was contained in that casual remark.

"Nothing else has been disturbed," Bryce announced, and included the whole room in one comprehensive gesture. "I'm going back to bed for a couple of hours. You young people can do just what you like."

He hustled us out of the room, shut the door carefully behind us, and went off to his room. Moira made no attempt to follow his example, but stood in the passage with her deep golden-brown eyes fixed on me. There was a look in them that I could not quite fathom; it whirled me back through five years of sorrow and stress, brought me back to the days when - . No, I wasn't going to think about it at all. It didn't bring me back to anything; it brought nothing back to me. Yet I could not help remarking that her eyes held solicitude for me and something that was more than that.

"Aren't you going back to rest?" I asked, and was surprised to note that there was both interest and defiance in my voice.

"I want to talk to you," she said, answering my question by inference. "I want to talk seriously to you."

So it was coming at last. She intended putting Bryce's advice into execution. Perhaps she thought it was merely a matter of telling me that she was sorry for what had occurred, and then everything would begin again just where it had left off. If she thought so she was radically mistaken. My love had been rejected and I had been wounded in my pride. Through four long years of repression the knowledge had rankled in my mind till now the very sight of her standing there and beseeching me with her eyes was more than I could bear. I would not have been human had I not felt the old wound pricking me again, and I certainly would not have been a Carstairs had the mere sight of her apparent contrition moved me to forgive her on the spot. I was quite willing to be friendly, I told myself, but by nothing short of a miracle could we regain the old footing. The worst of it was that something moved me to take her in my arms then and there and kiss away the tears that were very near her eyes.

"I don't know what to say to you, Jim," she said tentatively.

"There's no need to say anything, Moira." I tried to speak as kindly as possible, but somehow I think I failed. "I happened to overhear you and your uncle yesterday, and I know just what you mean. But, Moira, I don't see how things can ever be the same again. It isn't as if it were something I could forget. It isn't. It goes right down to the fundamentals. If our love wouldn't stand the strain I put on it, it wasn't worth having. I hate to have to speak to you like this, but, when all's said and done, it's just as well to be frank first as last."

She nodded with tight-closed lips. I saw that she was trying her hardest to keep control of herself, and for a moment it was touch and go with me. I very seldom set my mind to anything that I don't carry through, and in this instance I had a very clear and definite plan outlined in my mind. So I just set my teeth and carried it off as if nothing really mattered very much.

"You heard us yesterday then?" she said at length. She spoke so slowly that she almost drawled her words.

I nodded.

"That's what you were doing then when I came out of the room?"

"Exactly," I said. I fancied it would only make matters worse if I explained everything in detail.

"I was wrong, Jim, and I apologise," she said. There was a little gleam of flame in her eyes that made me hang on her words. "I was wrong," she repeated. "I said yesterday that you had changed, but I don't think you have. You're just the same old Jim, a bit of a savage and just as primitive as ever."

"Thank you, Moira," I said. "I didn't expect it from you, but now I know what to look for."

"It is war then?" she said, with a little sparkle in her eyes.

"War it is," I answered; "as the Spaniards say, 'Guerra al cuchillo.'"

"Please translate," she requested. "I do not speak Spanish."

"War to the knife," I said briskly.

She half turned, then spoke to me over her shoulder. "I had hoped that we would be allies," she said softly, and was gone before I could ask her why.

As was only to be expected, things were very quiet during the next few days. Bryce went about his own affairs more openly than hitherto. With the passing of our midnight visitor all fear of attack seemed to have disappeared. He did not say as much to me, but in many little ways he showed that he was much easier in his mind. I found that I had next to nothing to do. He did not go out of his way now to find something to keep me occupied. As a matter of fact, I saw very little of him and practically nothing at all of Moira.

I spent most of my time thinking. I went over everything that had happened from the moment I sat down on the beach right down to the visit of that interesting and entertaining gentleman who had made his exit from the house in so unorthodox a manner. There was logic running right through the piece; every little incident seemed to dovetail into the others, yet, because I did not have the key, I could not read the riddle. Why did the man on the beach fire at Bryce? I could not say. Then just for amusement's sake I got a piece of paper and a pencil and dotted down the items that wanted explaining. They ran somehow like this: -

1. Why was Bryce shot at?

2. Why was he being watched?

3. What was the meaning of those figures I had seen?

4. Why was Bryce so anxious to avoid publicity?

5. Why did everybody seem satisfied when the burglar got away?

6. What was the burglar after, and why was he apparently satisfied even when he got the wrong figures?

7. What did the piece of driftwood have to do with it, and what connection was there between the wood and the typed figures?

And, lastly, what was it all about, anyhow?

Some of the items taken singly were quite susceptible of explanation, but I could not put forward any solution that covered them in toto. So eventually I gave it up, deciding that it wasn't my affair, and the less I worried myself about what didn't concern me, the better.

* * * * *

The tragedy, coming as it did like a bolt out of a clear sky, so upset everything that I really cannot say whether it was a week or ten days later that it happened. But I do remember, with that accuracy of detail that a man sometimes retains even when he is doubtful of essentials, the various events of that evening.

Immediately after tea Bryce rose from the table with the expressed intention of going to his study. I recall that he remarked to Moira as he passed her that everything was going along swimmingly, and that if he had no further word during the next couple of days he would consider that it was quite safe to try his luck. I didn't understand what he meant, though he seemed to be referring in a general way to the late burglary, if burglary it could be called. Moira was quite aware of the drift of his remarks, for she asked him wouldn't it be better to let the week elapse before he did anything.

"We've waited too long," he said. "We should have got to work long before. Too much time has been wasted already." Then he turned to me and said casually, "Drop in and see me later on, Jim. I'll be working till about ten."

I told him that I'd be along very shortly, and then I went hunting for a book to read. I found one at length, and I got so interested in it that I did not notice time passing. I was brought back to reality by a quick step in the passage, and I turned my head to view the newcomer. It was only Moira on her way to the study. She went by me with her head in the air, as if I did not exist. I recall taking out my watch and noting that it was just a quarter-past-nine, and high time I went in and saw Bryce. However, as Moira had got in ahead of me, and her business was probably of a private nature, I decided to wait until I heard her come out again.

I turned back to my book, but had scarcely found my place when I caught the tinkle of breaking glass on woodwork, and practically at the same instant there was a sharp "pop," as if someone had drawn a cork from a bottle of some gaseous liquid. On the heels of that had come the single whip-like crack of a revolver. I swung to my feet in an instant, and the book dropped unheeded to the floor. During the last few days I had got out of the habit of carrying my revolver, but for all that I made straight for the study, and without the slightest ceremony turned the handle. The door was not locked; it opened at my touch. I doubt if it was even latched.

If my long years of training in the hard school of experience have brought me nothing else, they at least taught me to keep my head in just such an emergency as this present one. It was well for me that I had my nerves under complete control, for the sight that faced me was one that I could not have pictured in even my wildest flights of fancy. Bryce was slumped forward in his chair, his big head sunk on his chest. All the color had fled from his face, leaving it ashen pale. The kind eyes that used to sparkle so were glazed now in death, and squinted up at me through the tangled mat of his eyebrows. The whiteness of his immaculate shirt-front was defiled for the first and last time by the big blood stain that showed how his life had ebbed away. But it was Moira most of all who caught and held my attention. She was standing just a little to the left of Bryce, her deep eyes wide with horror and a smoking revolver still held in her white clenched hand. She was staring at Bryce and the blood-stain on his shirt as if what she saw was too monstrous for belief.

"Moira Drummond," I said, in a hard, cold, emotionless voice that I hardly recognised as mine, "put down that thing instantly."

She turned her head at my words and regarded me dazedly for just the fraction of a second. Then in an instant the revolver dropped from her nerveless fingers and clattered to the floor, she swayed like a willow-wand in the wind, and would have fallen had I not sprung to catch her. She went limp in my arms. I did not need a second glance to tell me that Bryce was dead, and that no one in this world could do anything for him now. So, recognising that my first duty was to the living, I turned my attention to Moira. She had merely fainted, and one or two simple remedies brought her round very quickly. She opened her golden-brown eyes and looked up into mine. The unaccustomed horror of what she had just gone through had not yet died out of them; they held a plaintive, pleading look that somehow went straight to my heart.

"I didn't do it," she quavered.

"Who said you did?" I asked.

"The way you looked and spoke to me, Jim - "

I stopped her with a gesture. "That's all right," I said consolingly. "I wouldn't have thought so for a moment. But tell me just what happened."

"That's more than I can," she said. "I was standing by him, talking, and suddenly I heard the window glass smash and something went 'pop.' And the next I knew uncle gave a little cry and his head fell forward on his chest. The blood was welling up out of his wound, and I saw that he was killed. His revolver was on the table, so I seized it and fired at the window. I don't know whether I hit whoever fired, but I hope I did," she concluded, with the faintest touch of forgivable viciousness in her voice.

It was only when she drew my attention to it that I remembered having heard the glass break. The window had a great big star in the centre of it with a myriad little cracks radiating from it like the spokes of a wheel.

Moira looked first at the window, then at the still figure sitting in the chair. Finally she turned to me.

"Jim, what are we to do?" she asked helplessly.

"Well," I answered, seeing now that everything fell upon me, "we'll have to get hold of a doctor. It's just for form's sake, you understand. He won't be able to do anything. Then we'll have to ring up the police. It's a blessing we've got the 'phone on, as I wouldn't care to leave you by yourself now even for a moment. It's a wonder that none of the servants heard the noise."

"They're all out, Jim."

"That's lucky in one way," I said. "Now, Moira, I want you to understand that the safety of us both depends on how far you back me up. We can't touch your uncle until the police come; there'd be trouble if we did. I'm going to ring up now, and in the meantime you'd better find some of your uncle's cartridges."

"Why, Jim?"

"I'll tell you when I come back," I said. "Just do as I tell you. There should be some in the drawer of that table. Be careful how you get them out; you don't want to have to touch anything more than you can help. I'll leave the door open so I can see you from the 'phone. You won't be frightened?"

She shook her head, but her white face told me as plainly as so many words that the sooner I came back the better. Accordingly I wasted no further time, but turned on the hall light and took up the telephone-book. For a wonder I had no difficulty in getting connected with either the doctor or the police, and, once I had made my meaning plain, I hung up and returned to Moira.

"The police'll be here in ten minutes at the outside," I said. "I've got just that time to make you word-perfect. You've got the cartridges? Thanks. I only want one. Now listen. Your story's thin, it's so thin that there's many a detective wouldn't believe it; but I'm not going to give them a chance. I'm going to rig up things so that they'll look right. What happened is this: - You and I were out in the next room, reading if you like, when we heard a shot. We rushed in and found your uncle just as he is now. We've no idea who shot him, and neither you nor I fired a shot. When we find your uncle's revolver in the drawer with its seven chambers undischarged we're going to be just as much at sea as anybody else."

"But I did fire a shot," she objected. "How can you get away from that?"

"Easy. First of all I take out the discharged cylinder. Then I clean out the gun. I mustn't forget to clean it out, because if I do and people examine it, they'll see that it's been discharged, and they'll begin to suspect. We mustn't leave the least ground for suspicion. Now, there's the gun ready loaded in all its chambers and as clean as the day it came out of the shop. Back it goes into the drawer, and it stays there until the police find it. You understand just what you've to do now?"

"I think I do, Jim. But, oh, you've got to help me all you can!"

"I will that," I said in a sudden burst of cordiality. "I want you to feel that you can rely on me right through. And if there's any questions asked just let me do the answering, and if you're asked anything, why just say the same as I do. You can't say anything else because we were together all the night."

"But, Jim, I don't see why we should have to deceive people like this. Why is it necessary?"

"Have you ever heard of the thing called circumstantial evidence, Moira? You must remember that I heard a shot, and ran into the room just in time to see you standing over your uncle with a smoking revolver. I know what happened, but the police mightn't look at the matter in the same light. There's plenty of other ways of explaining that broken window."

"I suppose you know what's best," she said with a tired little sigh. "But it all does seem so horrible. I wish I hadn't to lie so."

"There's worse things than lying," I hinted. "It's a case of choosing the lesser of two evils, and really, Moira, I think in his own peculiar way your uncle trusted me."

She nodded as if she could not trust herself to speak.

Then came the sound of heavy footsteps on the verandah, and the door-bell rang violently.

"That's the police, very likely," I said in a quick whisper. "Just keep your head and leave the rest to me."

She said no word, but the pressure of her hand on mine told me more than hours of speech.

CHAPTER VI

I TELL A LIE

The police had brought the divisional surgeon with them, and he made his brief examination while the sergeant questioned Moira and myself. My story was the simple one that I had outlined, and I must say that Moira played up well to my lead. She was naturally upset at what she had gone through, and the sergeant, I fancy, made allowance for this, and attributed any trifling discrepancies between our two stories to this fact. He was one of the politest officials it has ever been my lot to deal with, and he carried out his duties in a way that made me his debtor for life. I was not as shocked by the occurrence as I might have been. I had seen far too much of the rough side of life and the sudden side of death to have any other feeling than a rather natural sorrow at losing a man who had been something more than a benefactor to me; but I did not make the radical mistake of treating Bryce's death too lightly. I rather flatter myself that I mixed my sorrow and my common sense in just the right proportions. It was different with Moira; she was genuinely distressed, and made no effort to conceal it. It was the first time for many years that I had seen her so unaffected, and natural, and I must say that the sight brought out all that was best in me.

The sergeant took our names and then began a close personal questioning. He enquired into my past life, asked me how long I had been with Bryce, and then bluntly demanded to know in what capacity I was staying in the house.

"Mr. Bryce," I said, "was an old friend of my father's, and naturally there was always a welcome here for me."

I picked my words carefully, because I was in mortal dread that some stray remark might put him on to that affair on the beach. I knew that if he once got wind of that everything was up with us, and our hastily-built castle of cards would come tumbling to the ground. While I was thinking of this it struck me all of a heap that there was a chance of something leaking out about the burglar of the other day. The only thing I could see was to make a clean breast of it.

"I don't know whether this has got anything to do with the burglary the other night," I said casually.

"What's that?" the sergeant demanded.

I repeated my remark. "This is the first I've heard of it," the man said. "Why wasn't it reported before? It's over a week ago, you say."

"About that," I agreed, "but it was reported. Mr. Bryce went down himself to tell you." And here I looked warningly at Moira. She gave no sign that she had noticed my glance, but somehow I felt that she quite understood what was required of her.

"I don't deny he might have come down," the man ran on, "but all the same no report has reached us."

"That's mighty curious," I said with assumed thoughtfulness. "Now I come to think of it, it struck me at the time that you people hadn't followed the matter up. I meant to ask Mr. Bryce about it, but the matter went clean out of my mind, and it was just this moment that I recollected it. It does seem a bit of a puzzler."

"If you tell me all that happened, Mr. Carstairs," the sergeant suggested, " it might help us a bit. There's something very like a motive in this."

I gave him a rather sketchy account of the night of the burglar's visit, but, without actually giving a false description of the burglar himself, I so drew him that he would be difficult to recognise. I was swayed by cautiousness more than anything else at the moment, but I fancy that deep down in my mind was a primitive longing to settle with the man without having recourse to the law. At any rate no policeman in the country would have arrested him on the description I gave.

"It's a pity he got away," said the sergeant when I'd finished. "It looks as if he's the man. What was taken, Mr. Carstairs?"

"According to Mr. Bryce there wasn't anything even touched."

"Looks as if Mr. Bryce had a past," the man said in a half-whisper meant for my ears alone.

I regarded the suggestion with alarm. "I don't see how that could be," I told him. "I've known him for a good many years, and my father knew him before that. But of course I've been in the Islands for close on to four years, and something that I am unaware of may have occurred in that time."

"Just so," he agreed. "We'll see what Miss Drummond has to say."

"Had your uncle any enemies that you know of?" she was asked.

She answered the question with admirable adroitness. "My uncle was the kindest of men," she said. "I can conceive of no reason why he should have any enemies."

I suppose our very apparent frankness threw the man off his guard, for I'm perfectly satisfied that he could have tripped us up more than once had he had the faintest suspicion that we were not telling the exact truth. But we strove, rather successfully as it now appears, to twist the truth to suit ourselves without actually telling a downright lie, and we did it in a way that seemed to satisfy him, astute though he was. I told him but one lie that evening, though as a matter of fact it was much nearer the truth than anything else I had said, so strangely do things fall out.

"Miss Drummond is Mr. Bryce's niece, isn't she?" he asked.

"That's right," I said, and Moira nodded.

"Now let me see," he ran on, ticking off the points on his fingers, "you are an old friend of the family's. That's correct, isn't it?"

"That's so," I agreed.

"Anything more?"

"I don't quite understand you," I said, with the faintest doubt at the back of my mind. He spoke as if he knew or suspected something more than I had told him.

He looked at Moira and then at me, and I saw that he was smiling. It was just the sort of smile that one would expect from that portion of the world that loves a lover.

"Oh!" I said with a relief that I made no attempt to hide, "so you've guessed it."

"Guessed what?" Moira queried quickly, her face paling to a perceptible degree.

I turned to her with the cheeriest smile I could muster at the moment. "He's guessed that we're engaged, Moira," I said. And the note of exultation in my voice was more real than I had intended.

"It's not the time to be rejoicing over such things," I rattled on, "but - well, I suppose we're all young only once and we've got to make the best of it."

The sergeant was a gem of his kind, and even the nearness of a tragedy and the rigidness of the rules that governed his daily life had not crushed out of him that little touch of Nature that makes the whole world kin. Thanks to the easiness of my manner and his own ready stumbling into the trap I had not set for him, he now looked upon me as nothing more than a love-sick youth with no eyes for anyone or anything save the girl who occupied his heart. If the man could only have seen what was in my mind, if by any chance he had overheard our conversation on the morning of the burglary, how quickly he would have changed his good opinion of us both. But luckily he was no mind-reader, and my little piece of bluff achieved more success than was its due.

"You needn't worry about anything," he said with an almost paternal note in his voice. "We police have certain duties to carry out, but we're human after all, and anything I can do as a man and a brother I'll be only too pleased to have you ask."

"Thank you," I said, with gratitude that was less than half feigned.

The divisional surgeon gave it as his opinion that death had been practically instantaneous. The bullet had entered the wall of the chest a little too close to the heart to be pleasant. The doctor did tell me just what else had happened, but either he did not make himself clear or I have forgotten it.

Presently a couple of the police who had been put on the trail of the fugitive returned and reported nothing doing. The garden just outside the window was a good deal trampled about, and there were footmarks in plenty on the soft soil, but, as the sergeant remarked, "Footmarks are like finger prints - they're no use unless you know who made them." All things considered, it looked as if our man had got clean away again. I had a fancy that neither Moira nor I had seen the last of him.

Standing there in the very room that had witnessed the tragedy, with the body of the murdered man hanging limply in the chair, the lifeless clay scarcely yet cold, it came to me with something of the clearness of prophecy that this was not the end but the beginning of the play. It was something closely akin to second sight, and for the moment the spaciousness of the vision that I saw but dimly thrilled me with its possibilities. I knew, though how I knew I cannot say even at this distant date, that the calm, silent policemen with their helmets in their hands, the earnest, energetic divisional surgeon, and his confrere the sergeant, even the dead man himself, were but the merest supers in the prelude to adventure. Moira and I were the only ones who were real, the only actors that were something more than mummers. Yet even I failed to see that what had happened that night was something more than a queer insoluble mystery. There was nothing in my experience to tell me that it was vitally connected with the early history of Victoria, that it had its being in the now far-off days before Australia became a nation. I think if any supernatural whisper of the truth had reached me that I would not have been surprised, but that is the most that I can say.

I came back abruptly to reality to find a cold wind blowing in through the crack in the window. The doctor and the two policemen between them were lifting Bryce out of the chair he would never more occupy, and I, with my profounder knowledge of death and its consequences, saw just what they were going to do.

"I think I'd better take Miss Drummond outside for the present," I whispered to the sergeant. The man nodded, and, taking Moira by the arm, I led her from the room.

"It would be better if you could go to bed," I suggested.

She shook her head wearily. "I can't, Jim. It's no good trying to persuade me. I just couldn't."

"I think I understand," I said softly.

"I don't feel sorry a bit, Jim. I know it's a strange thing to say, but it's the truth, and there it is. I couldn't summon a tear. But just inside me there's a vacancy, a sense of loss. He's gone out of my life, and I'll never meet anyone who'll quite take his place. I can't put what I mean into so many words, but I think you can understand. You're quick at understanding, Jim. I don't feel sorry a bit, and I don't want to cry, somehow; but I'll miss him dreadfully. I'm hard in some ways, Jim. I must be terribly devoid of affection."

I made no answer to that. My thoughts were on one summer's evening four - or was it five? - years ago, and in the light of what had happened then I could scarcely contradict her now.

"I'm sorry," I said abruptly, "that I had to tell that lie about our being engaged. But I had to be as natural as I could, and the more obvious an explanation I gave the better for us all."

She looked at me for a moment with unutterable things in the depths of her golden-brown eyes.

"I'm sorry," she said slowly, "that you had to tell a lie."

I took her remark as the natural corollary of mine, but some sub-conscious sense in me insisted that its very ambiguity was designed.

Almost at that moment I heard footsteps in the hall, and knew that the servants had just come home. The big clock in the hall chimed ten.

"There's the women," I said. "You'd better tell them, and see they don't make a scene."

Moira nodded and went down the hall to meet them.

There is little more to relate of this phase of my story. Naturally there was an inquest, and just as naturally was a verdict returned of "death at the hands of a person or persons unknown," or words to that effect. The situation, in fine, was that Bryce was dead and buried, and the police admitted that they held no clue to the identity of the murderer. Motive there was none as far as they could see, and the whole affair looked like one of these senseless crimes that from time to time startle the city folk from their easy-going equanimity. The matter was not even a nine-days' wonder, for other things occupied the attention of the press, and a stickful was the most it ever got in any paper.

I stayed on in the house at Moira's request and attended to several matters that were rather outside her province. The old man turned out not to be as rich as we had thought, though he had money enough in truth. The bulk of this went to Moira, with the curious proviso that she could not invest it in any way without first submitting the proposal to me and receiving my sanction. The will was of recent date, as a matter of fact it had been drawn up within a few days of Moira's arrival. There was a sum left to me, too, enough to make me independent for a good many years to come.

Moira's mother arrived the day after the tragedy, and showed no very evident intention of returning home. She was very nice to me, but then there was no reason why she should have been anything else. Any strain that there had been, and was still for that matter, was between her daughter and myself, and, like a wise mother, she forebore from interfering in what did not immediately concern her.

For my own sake, if for no other reason, I hurried along the winding-up of Bryce's affairs. I saw, or fancied I saw, that the sooner I left the house the better would Moira be pleased. For when all was said and done there could be no denying that things were far from satisfactory. Neither of us made any further reference to my bare-faced lying on that ill-starred night, but the more I thought of it the more equivocal did the present situation seem. I for one was doubly glad when at last we finished with the lawyers, and things - blessed, indefinite word - seemed like to settle down again.

My time of departure was no further off than twenty-four hours away when the incident occurred that led to a hurried readjustment of my plans and that brought us, willy-nilly, to the Valley - for so I still persist in calling it, as if there were not another valley in the world - and the treasure that lay there and helped us to unravel the tangled threads of Bryce's past life.

I had my bag already packed, and had announced that I was going the next evening, when Moira stayed me with a word.

"I've been meaning to talk to you for a long time," she said, "but somehow I could never seem to summon up enough courage. It's about Uncle and ... well, you know as well as I do, that there was some mystery about him."

"Go on," I said.

"Well, he told me once that if ever anything happened to him we would find documents in his room that would help us to take up the work where he left off. He repeated that the very night he died. Don't you see what that means?"

"It means that they are still there," I said soberly.

CHAPTER VII

INTRODUCING MR. ALBERT CUMSHAW

"That's the peculiar part of it, Jim. They should still be in the room, because they couldn't possibly have been taken away. Yet I've hunted high and low and I can't find them."

"And, now you find you're in difficulties, you call me in," I hinted.

"Jim, I wish you wouldn't talk that way. There's no call for us to be continually bickering. If we can't be anything else, at least we can be friends, can't we?"

"I suppose it's worth trying. But what have the papers to do with me?"

"They affect you as well as me, Jim. Uncle wished the two of us to carry on his work."

"How pleasant!" I murmured. "And suppose I refuse?"

"Well," she said, with just the least gesture of helplessness, "I'll have to do whatever I can myself. But it was Uncle's wish that we divide the proceeds."

"The proceeds of what?"

"That's more than I can say, Jim. We've got to find the

papers first."

"That's so, Moira. Seeing it's you, I'll hunt for them; if it's worth while I might even help you through, but you'll have to understand from the very start that I won't finger a penny of what you call the proceeds."

"You usen't to be like that, Jim."

"I've changed a lot, haven't I?" I grinned.

For a moment she stared blankly at me, then she asked me, as if the thought had just occurred to her, "There isn't any other girl, is there?"

"There never was any other girl," I said. "There was always only the one, but she failed...."

I saw that she had some intimate little revelation on the tip of her tongue, so, for fear she might say too much - one never knows what a woman will say if she fancies any words of hers will gain the day - I said briskly, "Now, about those papers, Moira. Where did you look?"

"Everywhere, Jim."

"You couldn't have. There's one place at least where you haven't looked."

"And that?" she queried eagerly.

"The place where they're hidden," I answered disconcertingly.

"Oh," she said blankly; and then, "Have you any idea where that is?"

I shook my head. "None at all, Moira. Still your uncle told you that they were in his study, and as you say they couldn't have been taken away, the only thing to do is to look in every likely place for a start."

"And if we find nothing?"

"Then we'll look in the unlikely places. And as there's no time like the present, I suggest we start now."

Moira was quite agreeable to that, so we entered the room. Books and everything lay just as we had left them the night of the tragedy; only the broken window-pane had been taken out and a new one inserted.

"I never thought of it before," I remarked, "but the sight of that new pane just brought to my mind how narrow a squeak you had that night."

"I don't follow you, Jim."

"Well, if our friends the police hadn't been so willing to swallow the obvious, they would have seen that my tale was all bunkum. When that chap fired he starred the window, and when your shot went through it finished the job and knocked a finger of glass right out. If the sergeant had only gone over to the window and examined it carefully, he would have seen enough to make him wonder how the deuce the same shot could have hit the same bit of glass in two places. But he didn't go over to examine it; I had filled his mind with an hypothesis, and he couldn't see anything else but that. Now it's the same with this business of looking for the papers. You seem to think your uncle would put them just where anyone could lay hands on them. I don't. Your uncle had a fair amount of foresight - he realised all along that it was likely that he'd be cut off short - and the mere fact that he told you twice at least that he had left you instructions shows that he had gone about things carefully and methodically. Again, he had no means of knowing just how he would be killed, so you can take it for granted that he provided against such a contingency as this room being thoroughly searched by the murderers. In other words, the papers are so placed that only an intelligent person who knew your uncle's mind would guess where the hiding place is. Now I'm having a wild shot at it, but it's logical enough in all conscience. When you can't find a thing, try to take over the mentality of the man who hid it."

"I'm afraid you're getting too deep for me, Jim."

"I'll put it another way, Moira. Something influenced your uncle in the hiding-place he selected, and we've got to parallel his thoughts, if we can, in order to find out the spot."

"But that's impossible."

"At first glance it seems like it. But just think the matter over. I've got more than half an idea already. Whatever those papers are they're certainly typewritten, and I'm sure they've something to do with that bit of wood. Oh, I forgot. I've never told you about that. It happened on the beach."

"Uncle told me how he met you," Moira volunteered.

"I'll bet he didn't say anything about the driftwood though."

"No, he did not," Moira admitted. So then and there I told her the tale. "You can understand from that," I concluded, "that whatever he was typing had something to do with that piece of wood. Now when he had made up his mind to secrete the papers two words would be prominent in his thoughts."

"I know," she said with a flash of intuition.

"Tell me," I smiled.

"'Sands' and 'wood,'" she said eagerly.

"'Wood' is one of them," I answered, "but I rather prefer to say 'bury' for the other. Now the only place he could bury anything about here in such a way that it wouldn't be noticed is under the hearthstone; but, as it's cement in this case, I think we can leave it out of the question. He wouldn't put them under the floor. For one thing it'd take too long, and the sweepers would be sure to notice if the carpet or the linoleum had been disturbed. So that brings us back to 'wood' again."

"How about the wall? A secret panel, or something of the kind?"

"I don't think he'd select anything so obvious," I said with a shake of my head. "It had to be a place that we'd find, but that everyone else would miss. There's quite a lot of wooden articles here, Moira, so we'll go over them very carefully."

I surveyed the furniture ruefully. "Looks as if we'll have to chop a lot of things to pieces," I remarked.

"Silly!" said Moira Drummond disgustedly. "We're looking for something hollow, so why not tap?"

"Brilliant idea!" I said.

As I sit writing at this table in that very same room, the scene comes back to me with all the clearness of a well-developed photograph. In my mind's eye I see Moira and myself on our knees tapping every inch of the old mahogany and the newer imitation Chippendale, and I realise as I have realised a dozen times since to what needless trouble we went, when a little thought upon the lines that I have already mapped out would have led us just as easily, and perhaps a good deal quicker, to the very spot itself. But we were young then - though for that matter we are still - and to young people all motion is progress. It is only when one gets older and sees things in perspective that one realises.... But that wasn't what I set out to write about.

The long and short of it was that we tapped all the furniture most carefully, and at the end of it found that our persistence was still unrewarded.

"There's something wrong somewhere," Moira said disappointedly.

"It seems as if there's been a mistake in our judgment," I agreed. "Still I fancy the table's the most likely place. You see he sat there always."

"Suppose you sit in his place then, Jim."

"Excellent idea, Moira," I said, and at once proceeded to put it into practice.

"Now if I had just finished typing anything and was looking for a safe place to hide it, where would I naturally go?" I said out aloud. Moira dropped into a chair on the other side of the table and leaned forward, her chin resting in her hand, and regarded me with intense interest. I went on talking to myself. "I'm thinking of wood, and the nearest wood to me is the table. Therefore I'd hide it somewhere about the table, not in or on it, but just about it."

Moira's eyes glowed - I remember that particularly - and we both must have seized on the idea at one and the same instant.

"Oh, why didn't we think of it before?" she cried, and then the two of us were on our knees and groping under the table. It was a massive piece of furniture in its way, with a large cross-piece running from side to side underneath. And on this cross-piece, so tied with string that it could not slip off, was a tiny packet of oil-skin.

"The safest place in the house," I said, as I stood upright and held out a helping hand to Moira. "No one would ever think of looking there. See how nearly we missed it."

"Jim, Jim, let's have a look!" she begged.

My answer was to place the package in my pocket. "Not here," I said in explanation. "You must remember that those murdering gentlemen aren't accounted for yet, and it'd be a pity to let them get hold of the very thing we've been keeping out of their clutches for so long."

"I never thought of that," she said with a crestfallen air. "Of course you're right. But where'll we go?"

"Any of the inner rooms. The drawing-room, say. That hasn't got any windows opening out on to the garden."

Moira caught my arm. "Come on, Jim," she cried, "I'm dying to know what is in it."

"The more haste the less speed," I remarked soberly. "Likewise there's
many a slip between the cup and the lip."

"Don't, Jim, don't be pessimistic just when everything's beginning to turn out well."

"Beginning," I repeated. "You're right there. We're just beginning now."

But all the same she did not take her hand off my arm, and when hers slipped through mine in quite the good old way, I could not find it in my heart to tell her that she must do no such thing.

The drawing-room was just as comfortable a place as a man could wish, and I saw at a glance that there was no likelihood of our being disturbed there.

I held the packet in my hands for I don't know how many seconds, almost afraid to open it. Inside was the secret that had lost Bryce his life, the secret that had cost, though I did not know it at the time, almost a dozen lives, and that would bring two at least of our associates perilously close to the grave before our work was ended. Moira shared some of my hesitation, for she made no effort to hurry me into undoing the packet, but stood awaiting my pleasure.

The string was tied so tightly that I could not unknot it. I drew my knife and cut it, and the oil-skin unrolled of itself. The first thing I came across was a letter from Bryce addressed to the two of us. It was not contained in an envelope, but seemed to have been slipped in as an after-thought. It ran: -

Dear Moira and Dear Jimmy, -

If you ever read this it will be because I am no more and have failed to bring my plans to a successful conclusion. In that case I look to the two of you to carry on from the point where I left off, but because you are both young, and so have very little sense, I don't intend to let either of you fall into an easy thing. There's money at the back of this, enough to make you rich for life, but you'll have to use the brains you both have got and work like the very dickens to get it. I've put some of the necessary directions in a cypher that a child could read, but apart from that you'll have to use your heads. As you know some things that Moira doesn't, Jimmy, and vice versa, you can see that it won't pay either of you to quarrel.

The man who really holds the key to the situation is a gentleman named Abel Cumshaw. Abel, I understand, is in his second childhood, and can never be brought to realise that it is any later than the early eighties, but his son Albert is a most astonishing young fellow, as you'll find when you meet him, if you have not already done so before this falls into your hands. You see I have sufficient confidence in your ability to believe that you will find this package sooner or later. If it's too late when you do find it, of course the joke'll be on the pair of you.

Now, a word to you, Moira. Jimmy knows the hidden valley quite well, so don't believe him if he says he doesn't. I spent nearly an hour the other day telling him all about it, and even went the length of showing him a map of the place. If he doesn't help you out, it's because he's got a bad memory.

As for yourself, Jimmy, remember that you can't get along without Moira and don't try. Once you've found what you're looking for you can each go your own way, but I rather fancy you won't want to then. I think that's about all, unless to remind you that Mr. Albert Cumshaw will be entitled to his fair share of the spoils.

And on that note the letter ended, and underneath was his sprawling signature, "H. Bryce," written as firmly as ever he had written it.

"Well, what do you make of that?" I asked when I had finished reading it.

"I - I - "

"I know," I cut in. "I feel that way too. Do you think he's put up a joke on us?"

"I just don't want to speak about it," Moira said tearfully. "It's - it's - I wouldn't have expected it of him."

"It's the unexpected that happens," I said with some idea that I was consoling her. I could see that the tears were very near her eyes, and I didn't want her to break down now and cry. A man is always at a great disadvantage in dealing with a weeping woman; she can usually persuade him to do almost anything for her while she's in that state. If I find my wife crying - but it doesn't matter what I'd do, for I've no right to be introducing purely speculative matter that has nothing at all to do with the story.

"It doesn't explain anything," Moira said at length. "It only makes everything worse than ever."

"I wouldn't say that," I said. I saw, or thought I saw, a

glimmer of light. It was so faint that I daren't as yet put it into words. "He must have been in a rather frivolous mood when he wrote this," I continued. "All the same, I think we're getting closer. We haven't looked at the cypher yet, you know."

"No more we have, Jim. Let's see what it's like."

I handed it to her. At first sight I could have sworn that it was the identical piece of paper that I had picked up from the kitchen floor that momentous afternoon, but a second glance showed me that I was mistaken. Many of the characters were the same, but the grouping was altogether different. They ran as follows: -

> 2@3; 5@3 &9; 3 5433-3/4 5@3 @75 L994 1/4; L 5@3 48-1/2-8;? 1/2-7; 1/4-43 8; &8;3 - 3-1/4-1/2-743 1/2-3: 3; "335 3-1/4-1/2-5.5@3; "1/4-/3 L843/5 ;945@3/4 L4-1/4-2 1/4;95@34 &8;3 1/4-5 48?@5 1/4;?&3-1/2 59 5@3 043:897-1/2 9;3 3)53; L8;? "94 523&:3 "335.L8? 5@3.

"It doesn't seem to mean anything, Jim," she said in consternation.

"I'll admit it's pretty hard to understand," I told her. "It looks like a page out of a ready reckoner or a mathematician's nightmare. But it does mean something or your uncle wouldn't have put it up to us. What it is we've got to find out. Possibly the Mr. Cumshaw of the letter can throw a little light on the subject."

"Who is Mr. Cumshaw, Jim?"

"I never heard of the man until I read this letter," I said. "He's a new element in the plot, and, unless your uncle's pulling our legs, I think he's going to be a very important factor."

"He's got to share with us, too," she reminded me.

"Share with you," I corrected. "I've told you a couple of times already that I'll help you to it, but that I don't intend to take a penny of the money. So, when you're figuring it out, remember it's halves, not thirds, you're working on."

"If it was anybody else but me you'd take it quickly enough," she said accusingly.

"Maybe I would and again maybe I wouldn't," I said with a smile.

"Oh, Jim, I hate you!" she cried in a sudden blaze of temper.

"I'm sorry," I said easily. "It doesn't take much to make you hate seemingly."

She turned and faced me with one of those swift changes of front that made her so hard to deal with. The white-hot anger had gone as suddenly as it had come, and in its place there was nothing but hopelessness. She looked so weary and so miserable that for the moment I was tempted to take her in my arms and tell her that the past did not matter any more than did the future. But the memory of the words with which she had driven me out of her life that summer's evening long ago lashed me like a whip, and in an instant I had hardened my heart.

"Why do you make it so hard for me, Jim?" she moaned. "If only you would help me a little."

"I'm helping you all I can," I said with a touch of cynicism in my voice. "You can count on me until the adventure's finished."

"You know I don't mean that," she said weakly.

"There's nothing else you can mean," I answered stubbornly.

For the space of a heart-beat we stood facing each other. I saw that she was on the verge of a breakdown, and I knew that my own resolution was failing. After all, what need was there for me to be so brutal? She had suffered more than enough for the idle words spoken in haste all those years ago. There is no knowing what might have happened had not Fate intervened. But just as things had reached breaking-strain the door-bell rang. The prosaic sound brought us back instantly to earth, and a dramatic situation, tense with possibilities, became in a moment common-place.

"There's the door-bell," Moira said calmly. "I wonder who it can be."

"Some visitor or other," I remarked.

"What visitor could it be?" she asked. "I know of no one who'd have business here."

I knew of one at least, but I did not put my thoughts into words. Instead I remarked, "Quite possibly it's some house-hunter."

We heard the maid's steps go up the hall past us. There was a whispered colloquy at the door, and then, quite distinctly, the maid's voice said, "I'll see if he is in."

"That must be me," I guessed. "I'm the only 'he' in the house."

"But who knows you're here?" Moira objected.

"That's right," I said. "Who does?"

I opened the door of the room and looked out. The maid, who was coming down the passage, caught sight of me. "There's a gentleman wishes to see you, Mr. Carstairs," she announced.

"Show him in here," I said.

I turned back into the room. "You'd better stop here, Moira,"

I said as she made a movement to go. "It can't be anything private. It's just as likely that it's something that interests you too."

She sat down again.

The maid ushered the newcomer into the room. I ran my eye over him as I advanced to meet him. He was small and dapper, and his air of self-possession was almost perfect. His features were clean-cut, dark eyes glowed in a face that had evidently been exposed to the weather for many years, and his brow was surmounted by a mass of black curls.

"Mr. Carstairs?" he asked.

"That's me," I said truthfully but ungrammatically.

"This will explain my business," he said, and handed me a piece of pasteboard. I took it from him; it was one of Bryce's visiting cards, and scribbled across the foot of it were these words: - "Introducing Mr. Albert Cumshaw. H. Bryce."

"I've been expecting you, Mr. Cumshaw," I said. "I've been expecting you for some days now."

As a matter of fact I hadn't, but it is always a good rule to allow the other man to think you know everything.

"Moira," I said, "this is the Mr. Cumshaw we've been waiting for. Mr. Cumshaw, Miss Drummond."

"Pleased to meet you," he said and looked as if he meant it.

"Take a seat, Mr. Cumshaw," I said, and when he had accepted a chair, "What can I do for you?" I enquired.

He looked curiously from one to the other of us as if to seek an inspiration. "I presume Mr. Bryce is not about," he said at length.

"Well, hardly," I answered. "He's been dead this last couple of weeks." It was longer than that in reality, but I mentioned the first period that came into my head. Anyway, it didn't matter much how long it was since he died; nothing could make him any the less dead now.

"Oh," said Mr. Cumshaw quietly, as though my news was just what he had been expecting all along. "It is most regrettable," he added.

"Now what can I do for you?" I persisted.

"Touching the little matter of the gold escort," he said and fixed me with a glowing eye.

"Yes, the gold escort, Mr. Cumshaw. What about it!"

He did not answer that immediately, but eyed both Moira and me as if to test our receptive capacities. I maintained an attitude of complete indifference; Moira leaned forward a little with interest plainly marked in every line of her face.

"You were both in Mr. Bryce's confidence?" His quiet remark took the form of a question.

I nodded.

"Go on," Moira urged. "You came to tell us about your father, Mr. Abel Cumshaw."

"That's right," said the young man with amazing alacrity. "You're all right too. I wasn't sure at first, but now I see you're in the game with me. From what I know of it we're all like pieces of a jig-saw puzzle. We all fit in, and none of us is any use without the others. That being so, I fancy that we had better all place our cards on the table. Now which of you has got the cypher?"

Moira looked at me for guidance. I was pleased to see that she was learning that she couldn't do without me. I was pleased - no, I wasn't pleased at all, for it didn't matter now what Moira thought of me.

"What cypher is that?" I enquired innocently.

"There is only one cypher, Mr. Carstairs," Mr. Cumshaw stated. He seemed so sure about it that my curiosity was aroused.

"Indeed?" I said politely. I knew better than to contradict him outright, so I did it by implication.

"There's only the one," the young man repeated. "You should know, because Mr. Bryce left it to you."

If I had had any doubts before as to the genuine character of my visitor they all vanished at that last remark of his. It was one of those things that a man could not have guessed, however clever he might be. He must have had inside knowledge. Hitherto I had been indulging in that pleasant pastime that is known in boxing circles as "sparring for wind," but now I dropped the pose completely and answered him as straightforwardly as was consistent with reasonable caution.

"Yes, he did leave a cypher to me," I admitted. "But what do you know about it?"

"Only what Mr. Bryce wrote me. I'm sorry I can't show you the letter, but Mr. Bryce had an invariable rule that all correspondence from him must be burnt as soon as read."

"I guess I've got to accept you at your face value, Mr. Cumshaw," I said. "You'll pardon me for doubting you at first, but it pays to be cautious in a game like this. Now I'd like to know just how we are going to assist each other."

"That's more than I can say," the young man smiled. "If I tell you the story from start to finish, maybe you'll get a better idea of what we're after."

"Would it take long?" I said diffidently. "It's fairly late now."

"If Mr. Cumshaw would stop to tea," Moira suggested, and looked to me for approval of her proposition. Under the circumstances there was only one thing for me to do, so I did it.

"You'll greatly oblige us if you stop," I said. "That is if it won't be causing any inconvenience?" I added questioningly.

"None at all," he said cheerily. "Nothing of this sort ever inconveniences me" - this latter with a glance at Moira.

"So that's the game, is it, young man?" I said to myself. "Well, here's luck to you."

Aloud I said, "I am pleased to hear it." The funny part of it all was that I really meant it. There was something open and honest about the man himself, there was a healthful glow in his dark eyes, and he had a way of looking at one that was the very essence of frankness itself. Without knowing more of him than I had learnt in the few minutes we had been conversing, I felt that he was as open as the day. In this case at least my first impressions were more than justified by the course of events.

* * * * *

Mr. Cumshaw stopped to tea and made himself very much at home, and afterwards he told us the story of the gold escort. I have not set out his tale as we heard it that evening. For one thing he only related what he happened to know about the matter, and as a result there were many little blanks he had to leave unfilled. But with the completion of our enterprise many additional facts have come to light, and so it is that, with Mr. Cumshaw's aid and at his suggestion, I give here a fuller and more comprehensive version of the affair than he related to us that evening.

PART II

THE ADVENTURES OF MR. ABEL CUMSHAW

CHAPTER I

NIGHTFALL

Far away to the west the fiery globe of the setting sun dropped lazily down to rest behind the quaint goblin peaks of the Grampians. Its last lingering rays touched their summits with a crimson glow, flooded the valleys with garish light, and even penetrated into the recesses of the nearby woodlands until the whole place seemed to blaze as with the red fire of Hell. It was not a peaceful sunset; it did not even hold the promise of peace. It was alive and active, in the sense that light can live, and one could but feel that its potency was malignant and assured. There were clouds aplenty in the sky, light clouds looking as if they had been trailed through red ink, but there was nothing about them to suggest that a storm was brewing, or that even the slightest change in the weather could be expected. Nevertheless the air contained a hint of evil, so much so that an imaginative person would have peopled the hills with gnomes and the woods with devils. Even had fairies existed in the glades, one would have instinctively known them to be bad fairies. Yet one could not say offhand whence or from whom the evil that was to be, would originate; all earth and sky seemed somehow to be in the dread conspiracy.

The lurid hues of the sunset flared and faded into the drabber colors of twilight, the shadows swept down in phalanxes from the hills, and the still lifeless trees, stirring in the evening breeze, became black mocking shapes of infamy. The yellow disc of a moon, climbing up over the woods, took on the semblance of the leering face of a drunken man.

The two men who presently came riding along through the tangled fastnesses of what a couple of score years or more ago were the untenanted and, to a great extent, the unexplored depths of a Victorian forest, were very evidently unaffected by the grim fancies of the evening. They were not laughing certainly, and when they spoke it was in whispers, but the younger man hummed a music-hall tune under his breath. There was something rakish, not to say reckless, in the way the elder sat his mount. They went carefully, though, taking every possible precaution against making needless noise. Once the horse of the elder man stumbled and set a stone rolling down a declivity. Both men reined in instantly and listened until the echoes died away in the distance.

"You're as nervous as a rabbit, Jack," the younger man remarked when presently they resumed their journey. "Every little sound seems to startle you."

"There's no sense in taking chances, man," said the one called Jack.

"If it comes to that there's no chances to take."

"Only that of being caught and hanged, Abel."

"There's not much hope of that," Abel Cumshaw replied. "Gentry like ourselves are rather out of fashion now since they've squashed the Kellys. The country's quietened down a lot, and a 'ranger's supposed to be a thing of the past. As it is, there's never been bushrangers in this part of the State, and what hasn't been is the least likely to happen in most people's estimation."

"I'm with you there, Abel," Jack said. "But even that's no reason why we shouldn't go carefully. You must remember that we don't know this part of the State too well. That's the beauty of it, I suppose. Nobody knows it very much."

"It'll make pursuit difficult," the other suggested. "But what I can't understand is why the banks should send so much gold across country when there's the railway."

"The railway, friend Cumshaw, isn't the safest route. There's just as clever men working that as used to be working the stages. Moreover, this cross-country route's much the quicker way of the two."

"For which we may thank the Lord," said Abel Cumshaw, with cheerful impiety.

"Time enough to thank the Lord," the other retorted, "when we've finished the job successfully. All the same, I wish we had a pack horse."

"If we had brought a pack-horse," said Cumshaw, "we'd have had half the country-side wondering what the deuce was up. Like as not they'd think there was a new gold-strike on."

"And they wouldn't have been wrong in that," the other answered with grim humor. "But let's get to the business of the evening, Abel. I've got a good idea to put the pursuers off the scent, that is, if there's any pursuit."

"Out with it, then," said Cumshaw.

The elder man reined in his horse, and, leaning over, whispered in his companion's ear. As the tale proceeded a cheerful grin spread over Cumshaw's face.

"That'll do fine," he said gleefully. "You almost make me wish they do pursue us just for the fun of seeing them fall in."

"There's nothing to be gained by being foolhardy," the elder man warned him. "Now we can't afford to waste time. Let us get to work at once."

Without more ado he led the way down through the tangle of forest and across the open glades until they reached the narrow track that wound like a monstrous brown ribbon through the enormous gums. At the edge of the road they both dismounted and tethered their horses to convenient trees. Then, stepping very gingerly, and taking extreme care not to leave any footprints on the dusty surface of the track, they groped about on the roadside. Presently they both returned to the horses, each of them carrying an armful of heavy stones which they loaded carefully into the enormous saddle-bags that dangled one on each side of the saddle-flaps.

"That should about do it," Cumshaw remarked, when this was completed.

"I hope so," the other answered curtly. He sprang to the saddle, loosed the reins that had tethered the animal, and setting his spurs deep into its flank galloped up the track for a matter of a hundred yards or so, closely followed by his companion. Then they turned sharply off into the bush, designedly traversing the soft impressionable ground. The heavily-laden horses floundered in the soft soil, and gradually the pace dropped away from a gallop to a canter, and finally to a walk. When nearly two miles of this sort of country had been covered, the two men reined in and dismounted. Next they unloaded the stones from the saddle-bags and hid them carefully in the undergrowth. Cumshaw then proceeded to cut his thick blanket into strips, each of about eighteen inches square. There were eight of these strips in all - four he kept himself and the others he handed to his companion.

"It's a smart enough dodge, all right," the man remarked. "The only possible flaw in it is that there might be some gentleman present who's dealt with cattle-duffers in the past. If so, he'd be pretty sure to scent our little game, and block it."

"Let's hope for the best," said Mr. Cumshaw, cheerfully, looking up from his work with a smile that even the darkness of the night could not hide. He was systematically wrapping the squares of blankets round the hoofs of his mount and securing them in such a way that they would remain fast even during a wild gallop over rough country. The trick itself was an old one; it had its origin many years previous in Texas and Arizona when the raiding Indians made their horses walk over blankets spread on the ground in order to hide the direction of their retreat. The idea had been adopted and developed by the Australian cattle-duffers to meet the exigencies of the country they worked in. The trick therefore was by no means a new one, and there was just a chance, as the man Jack remarked, that someone might drop to it. But the false hoof-prints were an unprecedented addition that would probably keep the pursuers long enough on the wrong scent to enable the precious pair to "escape" and "cache" their plunder.

It was characteristic of the two men that once they had taken all precautions they quietly dismissed the matter from their minds and rode slowly back to the roadway with scarce a thought for the business in hand. Abel Cumshaw would have whistled had he dared; as it was he hummed softly to himself. The moon was now well up in the heavens, and its fitful light creeping through the leafy roof above, made gibbering ghosts of the swaying gums. Mr. Abel Cumshaw and his companion, Jack Bradby, had been brought up in the Australian bush, their nerves were as steady as a rock, and where others saw grim visions of fancy they saw only waving bushes and stripped gums. Though the present adventure was their first essay in ranging, both of them had lived by their wits, or rather by others' want of wits, for more years than were good for them. Singly or together they had run other people's sheep and cattle and made a lucrative, if dishonest, living at the game, and during their visits to the towns had made it a point of warped honor to pay their expenses with the ill-gotten gold of some duller fellow-creature. On top of it all they had a carelessness of life and a free hand with their easily-earned wealth that found them friends wherever they went.

Bradby pulled up suddenly and held up his hand in warning to his companion. Some faint noise had caught his ear, and, excellent bushman that he was, he would not rest content until he had located and defined it. Silently as a shadow he slipped from his saddle and dropped recumbent on the ground. With one ear to the earth beneath he listened. He remained in this posture for perhaps a minute and a half, then he rose abruptly and turned to Mr. Cumshaw.

"Horses," he said laconically.

"Must be them," Mr. Cumshaw replied with almost equal brevity.

Deftly, and without haste of any sort, each man knotted a red and white spotted handkerchief across the lower half of his face, leaving only the eyes and forehead visible. Then each tilted his hat so that the shadow thrown by the brim shrouded the uncovered portion of the face. Mr. Cumshaw, with the amazing simplicity of a conjurer, produced a pair of ugly-looking revolvers from apparent nothingness, while his companion slipped his holsters round so that his weapons were within easy and immediate reach. He did not, however, remount his horse, but threw the reins to Mr. Cumshaw, who draped them over his arm in such a way that they did not hamper his movements in the least.

* * * * *

The little group of horsemen, four, or perhaps five in all, clattered down the track as unsuspiciously as a man could wish. They were chatting quite easily, even joyously, of the thousand and one little matters that supplied their daily lives with interest, and nothing must have been further from their thoughts than what actually occurred. The bank that had sent them had departed from all precedent in parcelling out the gold amongst the messengers. It was certainly against the rather strict regulations of the bank, but the man who had instructed them had that contempt for rules and regulations which is the mark of a man destined to rise in the world.

"The expense of sending you," he had said, "is certainly no greater than that of the recognised method of forwarding by coach. The security of my method is even greater as you are not at all open to suspicion."

As a matter of fact, all would have gone well had not one of the chosen messengers been a little too fond of his nightly drink, and more or less inclined to talk when in his cups. True, on this particular evening he had exercised a kind of maudlin caution, but the tactics of Mr. Jack Bradby were of the sort to extract valuable information in the least noticeable way possible, and as a consequence the man, while keeping a strict guard of his tongue, at the same time let fall enough information to satisfy the curiosity of the 'ranger.

The first intimation the little cavalcade had of the presence of the knights of the road was when a shadow moved out from behind a huge gum and a clear resounding voice invited them to halt or take the consequences. With one accord the riders pulled up, one man swore violently, and the hand of another dropped round to his belt in a hesitant manner. But Mr. Jack Bradby had eyes like an eagle, for he cried sharply, "Put your hands up instantly!"

All the men shot their hands skywards with a precision that could not have been bettered by weeks of training.

"You look ever so much better like that," said Mr. Jack Bradby pleasantly. "Just keep still. I'd hate to make corpses of any of you - you all look so much better alive."

The humor of this was apparently lost on the captured ones, for they received it in silence, much to Mr. Bradby's disgust.

"Laugh when I crack a joke!" he roared. "Laugh, all of you, damn you!"

Somebody giggled in a half-hearted manner.

"That's no sort of a laugh," snorted Mr. Bradby. "When I say laugh, I mean laugh. I don't want you to bubble like that jackass did." He indicated the giggler with one of his ugly-looking revolvers. "Now laugh altogether as if you meant it. One, two, three; off you go!"

They all roared at that, but there was a lack of enthusiasm in their voices. Mr. Bradby, however, passed that over and proceeded to the business of the evening.

"Now please keep your hands in the same position," Mr. Bradby continued. "You've got quite a lot of valuables in those saddle-bags of yours, and I'm going to annex them. And don't any of you move a hand or foot or you'll be shot before you can say 'Jack Robinson.' There's men in plenty in among those trees, so don't play any hanky-panky tricks if you value your lives."

The scared horsemen with one accord glanced toward the trees that fringed the road. Mr. Bradby had stage-managed the affair with such consummate skill that they could only see the dim forms of several horses. The shadows were cast so that it was impossible to say how many there were; as far as the captives were concerned a regiment of cavalry might have been massed behind the trees for all they could say to the contrary. They had a feeling that unseen eyes watched them and invisible firearms covered their every movement. A solitary ray of moonlight, glinting for an instant on one of Cumshaw's revolvers lent color to this suggestion, so like wise men they surrendered to the inevitable and allowed the explosive Mr. Bradby to relieve them first of all of their weapons, and, when he had "drawn their teeth," as he succinctly expressed it, to rifle their saddle-bags for the little packages of gold that it was their mission to guard with their lives. Life at all times is dearer than gold, and the men realised that they were in a trap from which there was only one way of escape. They submitted meekly to their fate, saw the saddle-bags rifled without a word of protest, and, deceived by the shadows, watched what they took to be half a dozen men at least loading up with the gold. It speaks well for the dominant personality of Mr. Bradby that no one seemed to have suspected that only two men were concerned in the hold-up, despite the fact that they really only saw one man and the shadowy outline of another.

"Turn round, all of you!" Mr. Bradby commanded when the transfer had been completed. "Turn round and keep your hands in the air!"

Obediently, albeit clumsily, since they could not use their hands, the horsemen wheeled their mounts around, and Mr. Bradby surveyed the scene with satisfaction.

"You all look nice from the rear," he remarked. "Some of you've got real fine backs. Just you keep like that now and see what the fairies'll send you."

So silently that he might have been a disembodied spirit he turned on his heel, seized the reins Mr. Cumshaw threw him and vaulted into the saddle. As softly as two shadows the horses melted into the night, their muffled hoofs making no sound on the hard earth.

Ten minutes later one of the horsemen, grown tired of the unearthly inaction and suspecting something of what had happened, slewed his head round very cautiously. In a flash he realised the position and imparted his discovery to his companions.

"We can't follow them," the leader said. "We're unarmed. Furthermore we've got no idea which way they went. The only thing we can do is to get back to the nearest police station and report."

The man who had first discovered the absence of the bushrangers had been employing his time in examining the ground for traces of the gang, and very shortly he came across the tracks that the precious pair had made earlier in the evening. An exclamation from him drew the others to the spot. By the flickering light of a match they inspected the hoof-marks, and then the leader of the party gave vent to a snort of disgust.

"There's only two of them," he said. "What fools we've been!"

"They completely took us in," remarked another member of the party.

"That's so," agreed a third, "but we can't make people understand. If we tell them how two men stuck us up, we're going to look a lot of goats. I For one think we'd better keep the number to ourselves, or, better still, we might say that there was a big party of them."

One or two demurred at this, but the bulk of the party knew well the ridicule that the truth would attach to them, and the result was that between them a story carrying the marks of probability was invented, and, thus armed against the laughter of the State, the party set out for the nearest town.

In the meanwhile Bradby and Cumshaw had doubled back on their tracks and were heading for the Grampians. Though neither of them had explored the mountains before, they were quite satisfied from what they knew of the general formation of the country that there were gullies, even valleys, where an army might lie hidden. So confident were the two adventurers that there was no danger of pursuit that they did not press forward at anything like a reasonable speed. They took things easy. Somewhere about two o'clock in the morning they halted and removed the blanket-pads from their horses' hoofs. Mr. Cumshaw was just going to throw them into the bushes when Mr. Bradby stopped him.

"Don't do that," he said, "we'd better destroy them outright."

"How?" queried Abel.

"Burn 'em, I should say," Mr. Bradby answered. "You make a good job of it, and you don't leave anything behind. If you throw them away someone's sure to find them just when it's most awkward for you. No, Abel, burn them and hurry up about it."

So it came about that presently a tiny spot of light glowed like a red warning beacon from the lower slopes of the range. A lonely prospector, a few miles to the east, saw the spark and wondered at it. He knew that no one lived in that part of the country. The more he thought of it the more it puzzled him, though with the morning there came an unexpected solution.

CHAPTER II

THE PURSUIT

A body of mounted troopers left Ararat an hour or so before daylight the next morning, and by seven o'clock had reached the scene of the robbery. They had with them a capable black tracker who had figured in recent events in the Wombat Ranges. He was a silent individual who answered to the name of "Jacky," a name that seems to be the heritage of all blacks who serve in the police force. He quickly picked up the false scent, and the party turned east. It wasn't until the horses stumbled over the heap of stones that some brilliant intellect dropped to the trick that had been played on them. Then, with the better part of an hour to the bad, the party returned to the starting-point of the trail.

"Seems to me," the sergeant in charge remarked to his subordinate, "that they've laid this trail with a good reason. Now if a man wanted to put you on the wrong track, what would you think he'd naturally do?"

"Send us in the opposite direction," said the other promptly.

"Quite so," said the sergeant. "Now the false trail leads east, so it's only reasonable to suppose that they've gone west."

"That's so," the other agreed. "Get-up, you brute." The latter remark was addressed to the horse, which showed an inclination to drop into a walk.

"Here you, Jacky!" the sergeant called, and when the black came to him he said, "Those white men have gone this way," pointing westward. "Look out for their tracks, though I don't fancy we'll see any for some time."

The black grunted non-committally. He had much the same idea himself, though he could not understand how the white man had guessed. Still he knew enough of the white men to realise that they were very, very clever, and sometimes found out things that even the black trackers did not understand. The black went back to his work in silence. Presently he grunted again. His quick eyes had noticed a grey woollen thread stamped into the earth. He lifted it gingerly up in his hand and held it out to the police. The sergeant took it, examined it carefully, and then, without any comment, handed it round to the others. There was no need to ask what it meant. All knew without being told that someone had lately passed that way, and who could that someone be unless one of the rangers?

The black went back again to the trail, bending down close to the ground for all the world like a little dog following the scent of the chase. He turned sharply off into the bushes and the troop went after him. Here and there - wherever the earth had chanced to be a little softer than usual - one could see round depressions somewhat about the size of a saucer, and one patch of damp soil gave a remarkably clear imprint of the fibres of some material.

"Clever chaps, by George!" the sergeant remarked. "They've got brains among them."

"How's that?" queried one of the police.

"They've tried the old duffers' dodge of blanketing the horses' hoofs. Sort of thing that works, too, unless a man happens to have his eyes well open. Luckily I've stumbled up against this sort of thing before."

The other man, who had his own ideas about the matter, nodded his head, but otherwise made no comment.

About ten o'clock the troopers debouched from the trees into a low-lying stretch of land. One could not call it a gully; it was more of a depression, a fault in the earth due to some local subsidence. On the nearest ridge a prospector's hut was perched, from the chimney of which a wisp of smoke ascended. When one of the mounted men dropped from the saddle and opened the door he found no one in charge, though a dinner was merrily simmering away on the fire.

"Whoever he is he can't be far away," the sergeant commented. "He wouldn't leave his dinner unless he was handy. Have a look for him, boys. He might be able to tell us something."

The men scattered in different directions down the depression, and presently a shout from one of them announced that the prospector had been found. He came toiling slowly up the slope, side by side with his discoverer. He was a small wiry man, with a heavy iron-grey beard, and his age, as well as one could guess, was something near to sixty.

"You don't happen to have seen a body of men, horsemen, passing this way late last night or early this morning?" the sergeant queried.

"Nobody passed this way last night," the man answered in a colorless voice. "Why?"

"A gold escort was robbed yesterday evening," the sergeant said, "and we've got information that the robbers came this way."

The man turned slowly and studied the lower slopes of the distant range. He saw, or seemed to see, something that interested him, and he stared so long that the sergeant said impatiently, "Well, what about it?"

"I was just wondering," said the little man in the same colorless voice. "I was just wondering if that was them."

"If who was?" the sergeant demanded. "Out with it, man, and don't keep us waiting all day."

"Last night," said the man distinctly, "there was a fire up on those ranges. It wasn't a bush-fire. I know a bush-fire. It was just a tiny little glow from here. I thought it was a fire showing through the open door of a hut, until I remembered that nobody lived up there. It didn't last long; it must have burnt out in ten minutes or so, so I knew that it was started by some traveller. It wasn't a camp-fire and they weren't cooking anything."

"How do you know that?" the sergeant said quickly.

"How do I know that?" the little man repeated slowly. "It's easy enough. The fire was only alight ten minutes at the most, and you can't cook anything or boil a billy in that time, I know."

"The old chap's right," one of the troopers said in an undertone to his superior.

The sergeant nodded. He turned again to the old prospector. "You're sure you didn't see anyone pass this way?" he queried.

"No, I'm not sure," said the man. "I'm only saying that I didn't hear anyone."

"What do you mean by saying you're not sure that you didn't see anyone?" the sergeant asked curiously.

"When there's shadows in the trees," said the old man, "there's times when you can't tell whether they're men or not. That's what I mean. I'm only saying that I didn't hear anyone. I'd have heard horses."

"The man's a hatter," the sergeant remarked as the troop galloped off towards the ranges. "As mad as a March hare."

The other grinned cheerfully. "Still there's a lot in what he said," he answered. "Now that about the fire - "

"I wonder why they lighted it," the sergeant cut-in.

"Don't know," the other said. "What's the sense of worrying anyway? We'll know soon enough. But don't you think we should have brought the old chap along with us?"

The sergeant shook his head. "What'd be the good?" he said. "He couldn't do any more than he's done already."

He swung round in his saddle and faced the troop. "Now, men," he said, "we've got to put our best foot foremost. Those 'rangers are somewhere ahead of us, making for the mountains. Keep your eyes skinned, for you never know the minute we'll catch up to them. They can't have such a big start of us, and they're heavily loaded at that."

The troopers unslung their carbines and examined the loading, then, satisfied that every preparation had been made, they set spurs to their horses and cantered up the track that led to the ranges.

It was Mr. Abel Cumshaw who first discovered the pursuers. Early in the afternoon the two men commenced to ascend the mountains proper. Just before they disappeared into the belt of timber that fringed the slopes the younger man turned in his saddle and cast one last backward glance at the valley they had left beneath them. Far away below them, in among the misty shapes of the distant trees, he caught a glimpse of a collection of dark little dots whose unfamiliar look puzzled him. He called Mr. Bradby's attention to them, and that gentleman glanced at them in an offhand way and pronounced them to be kangaroos.

"Come on," he added in a different tone. "Hurry up with you there!"

Mr. Cumshaw had no intention of moving until he was fully satisfied in his own mind that the little black dots were really kangaroos. Something seemed to whisper that they weren't.

"They're not kangaroos," he said with conviction. He had caught the glint of sunlight on metal, a brass button of a man's uniform, or perhaps the polished barrel of a carbine.

"Oh," said Mr. Bradby, "so you've tumbled."

"They're police," Mr. Cumshaw stated. "That's what they are."

"Didn't you know that, Abel? I guessed it as soon as I saw them. I'd never confuse a trooper with a kangaroo. I only said that to - well, I didn't want to scare you unnecessarily."

"You needn't be afraid of that," said Mr. Cumshaw airily. "I'm in the game for good or ill, and I'm taking all risks equally with you. It's as much my funeral as yours."

"It doesn't matter whose funeral it is," Jack Bradby said impatiently. "We've got to get away and do it smart. You must remember that neither of us knows anything at all about this country, and it's ten to one that those infernal police have got a black tracker or some other imp of Satan who'll be able to follow us, even if we left as little trace as so many flies."

"Where are we heading for anyway?" Abel Cumshaw enquired as he spurred his horse alongside his companion's.

"That's more than I can say," Bradby retorted. "If we'd had any gumption we'd have explored the place before we took on this last job. But we hadn't the time, and that's all there is to say about it. It's my impression that this section of the State is as full of hiding-places as ever the Blue Mountains or the Wombats were. If we only keep up this spurt of ours we'll make a gully or a valley where we can hide for months without a soul being a whit the wiser."

"I hope so," said Cumshaw, in the manner of a man who has very grave doubts.

"Hold your breath for your work," Mr. Bradby advised. "You might need it all yet."

They had made good headway by this, and the path that they had picked out took them every hour deeper into the unexplored heart of the country. On every side of them stretched the unbroken fastnesses of the primeval wilderness, sheer precipices dropping suddenly into infinite space, jagged peaks towering dizzily into the misty vault of heaven, quaintly situated valleys so masked by timber and brushwood that one came across them only by accident. There is something in the naked face of Nature, in the sheer magnificence of incredible heights and the marvellous massiveness of big timber that somehow dwarfs man into insignificance and makes him realise the puniness of his strength. There was something in the scenes now opening up before the rangers that subdued them and beat them into silence. There was beauty in the sight, the soft eternal beauty of an unravished land, but over and above that was the suggestion that the travellers were fighting not merely against their kind but against the untrammelled forces of an all-powerful wilderness.

The time was early December, and the golden wattle in full bloom. From end to end the ranges were a blaze of color, near at hand deep gold, fading away in the distance into that hazy blue-grey peculiar to Australian mountains. Hour by hour the men rode on in silence, at times galloping down the slopes, at others crawling slowly and painfully up hills that stretched apparently to heaven, hills that yet dropped suddenly into space when one had almost given up all hope of ever reaching the summit.

They had lost all sight of the pursuers, though once Bradby

caught a glimpse of smoke far away to the east, smoke that he fancied came from the mid-day fire of the troopers.

They halted at sunset in the shadow of a clump of red gums and made the first meal since morning. As a result of a hurried consultation they decided to press on until midnight. But the horses were wearied with the rough and constant travelling, and it took the better part of two hours for them to cover a little under three miles.

"They've got to have a rest and so have we," Bradby said finally. "The pace is killing, and I'm quite satisfied that the police are taking it fairly easy. We've got scared over nothing. They might not even be on our track. At any rate I suggest we finish for the night and get what sleep we can."

Abel Cumshaw raised no objection to this - as a matter of fact he was almost falling from his mount out of sheer saddle-weariness - so a halt was called, the horses were unsaddled, the men unrolled their blankets and settled down to slumber just as the silver ghost of the moon flooded the place with its cool white light.

It was broad daylight when they awoke, and the sun was already high up in the heavens.

"Somewhere about nine or ten o'clock," Cumshaw guessed. "We've slept in, Jack."

Bradby ruefully admitted that this was so, but excused it on the ground that they would be better fitted for the day's work.

"I'm hanged if I like this game," Cumshaw growled as they made a meagre breakfast on almost the last of their rations. "The food's running short, and it's only a matter of time until they wear us down. You know what it means for us, Jack, if they catch us with the gold. Now I've got an idea, and if we carry it out I see a chance of escaping scot-free.

The gold's weighing us down, so what we've got to do is to get rid of it."

"You're surely not going to throw it away after all we've gone through," said Bradby, aghast at the proposal.

"No, I'm not," Cumshaw told him. "What I suggest is that we hide it somewhere handy, make a note of the spot, and then clear out of this particular section for a time. We can easily keep afloat for a couple of months, and when the hue and cry has died down, we can come back and dig it up at our leisure. We'll gain nothing by sticking to it now and we'll run a chance of losing everything."

"Not a bad idea," Bradby agreed. "But the trouble's to find a suitable spot."

"We passed dozens of such places already, Jack. We're just as likely to strike something as good or even better during the course of the day. The whole country-side is honeycombed with hiding-places; it's like a rabbit-warren."

"There's nothing like being an optimist," Bradby said. "Have it your way, Abel. Now the sooner you find some nice secure little spot the better for us, I'm thinking. For one thing the food's running short, as you just remarked, and for another I don't intend keeping up this dodging game for ever. We can't last; they'll wear us down."

"That's supposing they don't get tired and go home," said the cheerful Mr. Cumshaw.

"Not much chance of that," Mr. Bradby retorted. "I only wish they would."

During the morning Bradby's horse developed lameness, and, though the two men slackened the pace in order to give it every chance, by mid-day it could barely limp along.

"This won't do," said Bradby in despair. "We're losing time we can ill afford. All the same this old crock'll have to struggle on until nightfall, and then we'll see whether we'll have to shoot it."

"I don't like shooting a horse," Cumshaw remarked. "It's like murder."

Bradby's only answer was a muttered oath. The trials of the Journey were bringing out the worst side of the man, a side that Cumshaw had never seen before. He eyed his companion thoughtfully. If the wilderness was to get on Bradby's nerves at this early stage, Cumshaw could see that there was likely to be very serious trouble before the end came. The air in the highlands was laden with a freshness which, while it stung the men to action, at the same time put a keen edge on their tempers. Both of them were children of the warm, sun-kissed lowlands, and the difference of even a few degrees of temperature had a remarkable effect on them. With Abel Cumshaw it was such as to send a warm glow into his cheeks; the cold bite of the air made his blood sparkle like new wine and urged him on to fresh efforts. It affected Mr. Bradby in another and a worse way. He became sullen, and there was a certain marked vindictiveness in the way he spurred his lame horse on to exertions that were plainly too much for it. Once or twice Abel was on the point of remonstrating with him, but for the sake of peace he held his tongue and waited, in the hope that the day would bring forth some measure of relief. But nothing happened that morning, and the hope died within him.

Late that day, when the pace had slowed down almost to a crawl, they stumbled across the place by the simplest kind of accident. They had been dropping down to lower levels the greater part of the day, and somewhere about three o'clock in the afternoon - they were not quite sure of the hour, since the sun was masked by the trees - they found themselves in what looked like a narrow gully. Both sides of it were lined with thick bushes of golden wattle that shut out all view on either hand. There were shadows galore in this narrow gully, and the place itself looked almost as dark as the entrance to the Pit. Cumshaw, who had a classical education and had not been able to forget it, any more than the fact that he had once been a gentleman, murmured under his breath.

"What's that?" Bradby asked sharply.

Cumshaw repeated his quotation. "Facilis est descensus Averno," he said.

"What does that mean?" Bradby enquired, in the tone of a man who imagines he is being insulted in a language he does not understand.

"It's easy to go to hell," Cumshaw translated.

Bradby shot one sharp curious glance at him, but made no comment on what he had said. They rode on in silence.

Presently they came to a patch of ground that had been broken by the wind or the rain, or perhaps both together. The shadows so fell that the travellers did not realise the treacherous nature of the soil until they were right in the middle of it. Cumshaw's horse floundered and would have fallen on its knees had he not reined in sharply. This caused him to cannon into his companion's mount. Bradby pulled back sharply, in some way jarring his animal's sore leg as he did so. It reared up on its haunches with the pain, and in the most approved manner bucked its rider off. He shot up in the air, described a beautiful half-circle, and sailed through the barrier of wattle like a human projectile.

Cumshaw slipped off his horse with the quickness of thought. He had enough presence of mind to tether both his own and Bradby's mount, and then he cautiously parted the bushes. For the moment he could see nothing but a great wall of golden blossoms, and then out of the depths came Bradby's furious voice. He was cursing the horse and the slope and everything and everyone within hearing in the simple and forceful fashion of the Australian bushman.

Cumshaw called to him and was answered with an oath.

"Where are you?" he repeated.

"Down here," said the voice, this time modifying its language. "Step carefully or you'll come a cropper."

Mr. Cumshaw pulled the bushes apart and found that he was standing on the verge of a sheer descent.

"Mind your eye," said the voice of the still invisible Mr. Bradby. "I've found the very place we've been looking for."

CHAPTER III

THE HIDDEN VALLEY

Abel Cumshaw caught at the bushes to save himself from slipping and turned a curious eye on the scene before him. Really there wasn't very much for him to see. Bradby had fallen into a miniature valley so small that it looked like the creation of a child. The place was heavily timbered, and almost all definable features were masked beneath the trees. Abel saw even in the first glance that here was just that ideal hiding-place for which they had been searching. Softly and cautiously he commenced to descend. The slope was slippery with green grass, and he finished the last few yards with a run. He came down amongst a lot of bracken and fern, and suffered no worse harm than the shock of a sudden stoppage. Mr. Bradby, he saw, was sitting almost buried in a mass of bracken, and looking much cheerier than his recent utterance would seem to suggest.

"Are you hurt?" Cumshaw asked him. He held out a helping hand. Mr. Bradby struggled to his feet and smiled at his questioner.

"Hurt? No," he said. "Only surprised. Why, Abel, here's the very place we want. We could hide here for years, and they could be scouring the country for us, and them not a penny the wiser. That tumble of mine was just the luckiest thing imaginable. You talk about falling into hell! Why, man, we've fallen into heaven, and if we don't make the best use we can of the place we're the biggest duffers alive."

"How are we to get the horses down here?" queried the practical Mr. Cumshaw.

Mr. Bradby eyed the slope down which he had come so precipitately, and then pursed up his lips.

"It don't look so easy from here," he said at length. "And from what I can see this place is walled in all round."

"Whether it is or not," said Cumshaw, "we've got to get those horses down, and get them down at once."

"But how?"

"That's what we've got to find out," said Cumshaw. And with that he commenced to climb up the slope again. It was hard work, much harder than coming down, but in the end he managed it. When he reached the top he turned, to find that Bradby was almost at his heels. He surveyed the place with the eye of a trained bushman; then he said, "We can manage it, Jack. It's a case of sliding them down, but once we get them started they'll go right enough."

"We'll give it a try," said Mr. Bradby. His usual good humor was fast re-asserting itself now that they had reached a haven of comparative safety, and he was ready to try any scheme that promised even the smallest chance of success.

Without wasting any further words on the matter the two men scrambled through the bushes and made their way towards the horses. The lame animal had quite recovered from its fright, and suffered its owner to lead it up the slight rise to the wattles, though there it drew back as if conscious of the drop beneath. But by dint of prodding and coaxing Bradby forced it through the crackling brush, and then, with a wild whinny of fear, it lost its footing and slid down the slope in an avalanche of grass and twigs. Cumshaw's mount made the descent in fine style, and the two men followed.

"Now," said Bradby, when they stood once more on level ground, "the further we get into this timber the better, I say. I don't suppose any passer-by would be likely to notice that we've come down here, do you?"

"All things considered," Mr. Cumshaw said slowly, "we've made little mess. We've got to thank that grassy slope for that. If it had been dry earth there'd have been tracks enough in all conscience. Yes, I think we can reasonably say that we've no need to fear anything - unless accidents."

As near as they could judge the valley was about a mile across at its widest, but it merged so gently into the further side of the ranges that it was almost impossible to say exactly. The wood grew thicker as the men advanced, until presently it was with difficulty that they could make their way forward.

"Getting pretty close," Bradby said at length.

Cumshaw nodded. He was too busy thinking over certain little peculiarities of the wood to take much notice of his companion's remarks. His quick eye had seen little cuts in the trees, bits of bark that had been chipped off here and there, and the sight set him wondering. The cuts were curiously like the blazing of a trail. They were regular, they were all about the same height on the tree-trunks, and they looked as if they had been made with an axe, not the crude stone weapon of an aborigine, but the sharp steel axe of a white man. Yet the place seemed deserted, and in all the air was that sense of utter desolation and absence of life that only those who have lived close to Nature can feel and understand.

"We're not the first here," Cumshaw said suddenly.

Bradby turned on him in alarm. "What d'y' mean?" he asked indistinctly.

"Some of the trees are blazed," Cumshaw pointed out. "The cuts are clean, and that means they've been done with an axe. But they're all weather-worn, so it must have been some time ago."

"I don't like the look of it all the same," Bradby said despondently. "It means that someone else has stumbled on this place - it doesn't matter much whether it was yesterday or ten years ago - and what has been done before will almost certainly be done again. If those troopers come this way - "

"What's the good of crossing the bridge before you come to it?" Cumshaw interrupted. "We've been lucky so far, and who's to say our luck won't hold out till the end?"

"It's the end I'm looking at," Bradby said gloomily. "It might be the sort of end neither of us'd fancy."

Mr. Cumshaw made no immediate reply. He was peering very intently through the boles of the trees as if he was not quite sure that what he saw was really there.

"What are you looking at?" Bradby demanded irritably.

"If that's not a bit of a clearing and a hut on the edge of it, I'm a lunatic," Abel Cumshaw said.

"Hell!" ejaculated Bradby, and he in his turn peered through the trees.

"There's no smoke coming from it," Cumshaw said comfortingly. "It looks deserted. I daresay it's been like that for years."

"I don't like this place," Bradby remarked with naive irrelevance. "It fair gives me the creeps. There's spooks about here."

"If you talk that way," said Cumshaw fiercely, "I'll put a bullet through you. That sort of talk's only fit for children. You're not a child. You ought to have more sense. There's things here doubtless that you and I don't understand, but they're quite capable of a rational explanation, so don't go digging up any stuff about ghosts until you find you can't explain them any other way. There's the hut in front of us, and either there's someone in it or there isn't. If there is, we've got to use our wits; if there isn't, the game's ours."

"Have it your own way," said Bradby. "I'm game enough when I know what I'm tackling. I only mentioned I didn't like the feel of the place, and I don't see that that gives you any call to say what you have."

"We'll call it off until we've investigated," Cumshaw replied. "You stay here with the horses, and I'll creep forward a bit and see if anyone's home. All the same, I'm willing to bet that the place's deserted."

"Maybe it is and maybe it isn't," suggested Bradby. "However, you go off as you say and I'll wait here for you."

Abel Cumshaw threw the reins to his companion, slid his revolver holsters round to the front within easy reach, should he need the weapons they contained, and slipped through the trees with the silence of a marauding tom-cat. Bradby watched him with some misgiving. No man could say with certainty just what secret the dilapidated hut held, and Bradby's state of mind was such that he took the gloomier view of the situation. He would not have been very much surprised to see half a dozen troopers issue from the hut. He would have taken it as the inevitable ending of such an adventure. He failed to understand the natural cheerfulness with which Cumshaw faced the situation. He was bright and volatile enough himself when dealing with the ordinary man - his courage was of that average quality that is always at its best when exercised before an admiring or frightened audience - but the abnormal brought home to him his own futility of purpose and his natural helplessness. While realising all this he was not man enough to rise above and overcome the limitations of his spirit.

Cumshaw swung round the corner of the hut and out of sight. Then it was that Bradby began to feel absolutely deserted, and the queer oppressiveness of the place descended on him as one shuts down the lid of a box. He was not the type of man who finds companionship in animals, and the nearness of the horses in nowise mitigated his fear. For he was afraid, unashamedly afraid, though of what he could no more have said than he could fly. He knew without understanding how the knowledge came to him that the valley was filled with the ghosts of dead things, dead trees, dead leaves, and perhaps dead hopes. His nerve was going; the intolerably close atmosphere of the wood brought little beads of perspiration out on him, and when he brushed his forehead with a trembling hand he was surprised to find it wet.

The horses stirred uneasily, and the lame animal gave a low whinny.

Then in the next instant the eternal silence of the valley was broken by a human voice. The suddenness of it startled Bradby, and it wasn't until he saw Cumshaw waving to him that he realised that the sound he had heard was his companion's "Coo-ee." He loosed his hold on the reins, allowing the two horses to wander where they might, and commenced to run towards the hut. Even as he ran his faculties collected themselves, and when he reached the corner of the hut he was almost his own man again.

Cumshaw eyed him curiously as he pulled up. "Startled you a bit, didn't I?" he said.

"I thought something had happened to you when I heard you call," Bradby answered, a trifle untruthfully.

"Don't you worry about me," Cumshaw said with affected unconcern, though something in the man's nervous tone troubled him in a way he could not define. "I've found the old chap who made the marks on the trees," he ran on.

"Where?" Bradby demanded. But he looked towards the hut-door apprehensively.

"He's in there," Cumshaw said, following the other's glance, "but there isn't anything to worry about. He's as dead as a door-nail."

"Dead," Bradby repeated dazedly.

Cumshaw nodded. "This many a day," he said in semi-explanation. "But come in and see what there is to be seen."

As if perfectly sure of his companion's acquiescence he turned and walked into the hut. After a moment's hesitation Bradby followed. The place smelt a trifle musty, and all the air was full of the subtle reek of decay. It was rather dim in the hut, and at first Mr. Bradby could see nothing but some indefinite shapes that might be anything at all. Gradually his eyes accustomed themselves to the gloom, and in the farthest corner he spied a rough bed of planks.

"That's him," said Mr. Cumshaw irreverently, and stirred something with his foot.

Mr. Bradby looked a little closer this time. The something that Cumshaw had stirred turned out to be the whitened skeleton of a man. The hideous thing about it was that it was not stretched out on the plank bed; it was propped up, as if the man had died while sitting. A rusted gun lay in line with the thing's left thigh, and Bradby, following the muzzle with a trained eye, saw that it was pointed at the man's head.

"Suicide," said Cumshaw. "Look at his head. He's blown out what little brains he had."

He was right. The frontal bones of the skull were shattered and twisted by the force of the charge; they gave the rest of the face a ghastly, leering look which turned Bradby physically sick. The other man was evidently troubled by no such qualms, for he loosened the gun from the bony hand that had clung to it so desperately through all those years, and tumbled the skeleton itself on to the plank bed.

"I'm going outside," said Mr. Bradby suddenly, and disappeared through the doorway with suspicious alacrity.

Mr. Cumshaw laughed softly. "Weak stomach," he murmured. "Well, someone's got to clear this old chap out, and, as it's certain to be me, I might as well do it first as last."

At that he gathered the white, clean-picked bones up in his arms, carried his burden through the doorway, and deposited it carefully on the grass outside the hut. His eye lighted on Mr. Bradby, who was sitting on the ground some distance away, looking very pale, and having all the appearance of a man who had reluctantly parted with his lunch.

"What the deuce are you doing?" he asked in tones that betrayed a certain amount of trepidation not unmixed with vague horror.

"Evicting the late tenant," Mr. Cumshaw grinned with cheerful inconsequence.

"Why?"

There was more than a question in the quick monosyllable. It contained also a hint of protest.

"Because we're going to camp inside the hut, and two's company and three's more of a crowd than I like. This old chap can stop out here for the night; I don't suppose he'll mind it much. If he's gone to the Abode of the Blessed he'll be above worrying over such mundane matters, and if he's anywhere else he'll be too much occupied to do anything but attend to the burnt spots."

"You shouldn't speak like that of the dead," Bradby said solemnly. "It's not right."

"If we stopped to consider whether a thing was right or wrong before we did it," Cumshaw retorted, "you and I wouldn't be here this evening. If you're wise, you'll leave all that talk till morning. The shadows are closing in, and we'll have the night on us before we know where we are. I'd suggest that we catch the horses while the light's still good. You must remember they've got those saddle-bags on them still. Of course, there's just enough food to make a meal for a pair of small-sized tom-cats, but I fancy we'll manage on it till morning. Who knows what we may find then? Perhaps a kangaroo, or at the worst a native-bear."

Bradby rose reluctantly to his feet, and, with a nervous glance at the remains of the unknown, followed his partner in crime. The horses had not strayed far; they were busily cropping the grass, and seemed quite content with their lot. The two men unloaded the saddle-bags and carried the contents into the hut. Then they hobbled the horses and turned them loose for the night.

The shadows were gathering in by this, and already the trees were full of misty shapes that had no relation to fact. The bulk of the hills shut out the last rays of the sun, though the western sky was still faintly tinged with crimson. Just as they entered the hut Cumshaw paused for a moment and ran his eye over the scene. The place seemed peaceful enough, but he had that queer sense of the bushman, a sense almost amounting to an instinct, that told him that there was trouble ahead. He shook the feeling off almost immediately and entered the hut. Bradby, despite his dislike of the conglomeration of bones on the grass outside, lingered a second or so longer. There was a light in the eastern sky, perhaps a faint reflection of the glow of the dying day, that lit up the hump of the nearest hill. It was practically bare of vegetation; only a solitary tree stood a lone sentinel on its very summit, showing black against the horizon.

The thought that sprung into Bradby's mind at that was that here was a landmark which there could be no possibility of mistaking. Already certain plans were germinating in his brain, and he saw, or fancied he saw, a way of turning this latest discovery to practical use. The bleached bones in front of him, too, became a means to an end, and, with the smile of a man who sees the way suddenly made clear, he too entered the hut in his turn.

Cumshaw was busily engaged in laying a fire in the centre of the hut, taking care, however, that its glow would not show through the open doorway. He looked up as Bradby entered and said, "I think we're safe in starting a fire here. It can't be seen by anyone crossing the hills, though there isn't much likelihood of that, and all the smoke we make won't do us any harm. There's always a certain amount of mist in a place like this, and a man a mile away wouldn't be able to tell the difference."

"Go ahead," said Mr. Bradby quietly. "You know what you are doing."

The compliment in the last remark was desperately like an insult, but Cumshaw did not seem to notice anything out of the way, for he bent down to his work and whistled cheerfully while he coaxed the fire into a blaze. Presently it was burning brightly, the billy was filled with water from the water-bottle, and tea was in a fair way of being prepared. "Great place, this," Cumshaw said presently.

"Great place," Mr. Bradby assented. "A man can die here without anyone being any the wiser."

Mr. Cumshaw made no reply to that, but the corners of his mouth tightened as if he suspected some hidden meaning beneath that smooth remark.

CHAPTER IV

WHEN THIEVES FALL OUT

Just as the first rays of the rising sun slanted into the hut Mr. Bradby stirred uneasily, threw out one arm, rolled over on his side, and in an instant was wide-awake. He sat up abruptly and gazed around. Abel Cumshaw was still sleeping peacefully, his head pillowed on the saddle-bags that contained the plunder. Mr. Bradby smiled grimly at the sight. Softly, without waking his companion, he rose from his rough bed and glided to the open doorway. He stood there for a moment, drinking in the fresh morning air.

The sun was just coming up behind the solitary tree that had so interested him the previous evening, and he noticed that from his position in the dead-centre of the doorway the sun and the tree were right in line. Again that curious, humorless smile flickered about the corners of his mouth. He stood meditating for a minute or so, then, with an assumption of carelessness that he did not feel, began pacing due east. He had not taken half a dozen strides before he turned at right angles to his previous course, and just as nonchalantly continued his stroll northward. This time he covered about double the distance, then stopped short and scratched a cross on the ground with the toe of his boot.

When he returned to the hut Abel Cumshaw was just getting up.

"Hallo, Jack," he greeted Bradby. "Been stirring long?"

"No," said Bradby shortly. Then, perhaps fancying his tone was a little too abrupt, he continued, "I've just been for a bit of a tour round."

"What do you think of the place?" Cumshaw asked casually. But he did not look up at his mate; he kept his eyes studiously on the ground.

"Just the sort of place we could make our headquarters," said Bradby, with an enthusiasm that even the forced restraint of his tone could not hide.

"I don't think we'll have much need of headquarters once this is over and done with," Cumshaw hinted.

"Maybe not," Bradby replied.

Cumshaw turned to the plank bed and lifted up the saddle-bags, one in each hand. "Don't you think we should get rid of these?" he remarked.

"I'd almost forgotten about them," Bradby answered with an assumed indifference. "Yes, we'll 'tend to them as soon as we've had something to eat."

"While you're talking about something to eat," Cumshaw told him, putting the bags down again, "I'd like to remind you that we're right on the last of the tucker. There's just enough flour for the day."

"I wouldn't worry about that," Bradby said. "There's sure to be plenty of game about in a thickly-wooded country like this."

Cumshaw nodded and dropped on his knees beside the embers of the evening's fire. In a few moments he was busy coaxing them into a blaze. Bradby stood behind him, watching the sweep of his shoulders with calculating eyes. Once his hand strayed almost unconsciously towards his revolver, then, with a gesture, half of horror, half of dismay, at the significance of his action, he twisted on his heel and strode to the door. He turned then, blocking the light with his figure, so that his face was just a black expressionless mask.

"It wouldn't be a bad idea," he suggested, "if I looked about for a likely spot to bury that stuff."

"Go ahead," said Cumshaw coolly, as if it were the most natural suggestion in the world.

Without further parley Bradby walked over to the spot he had marked earlier in the morning. Bending down, he commenced to dig in the soft soil with the point of his sheath-knife. The ground was easily enough worked, and in less than half an hour he had excavated a hole of close on to three feet in depth. He deepened it another six inches or so, and then stood up with a smile of the utmost complacency on his face.

"Nice spot you've chosen," said a voice at his elbow. He started at the sound. He had not heard Cumshaw approach, and the idea that his mate could come and go in such absolute silence filled him with dismay. Already the gold fever had seized hold of him and made him suspicious of every untoward move. Perhaps he fancied that some similar plan to his own was evolving in Cumshaw's brain.

"Yes, it is a nice spot," he answered. "It's easy enough to find once you know where it is, but it isn't the kind of place a stranger would blunder on."

Cumshaw eyed the hole in the ground, and then looked towards the hut, as if taking his bearings. Bradby noticed him and interposed hastily, "I've got the measurement of the place. Have you a piece of paper I can write it down on?"

Cumshaw ran hastily through his pockets. "I haven't a bit," he declared.

"Neither have I," said Bradby. "However, we'll have to keep it in our heads. It's just ten feet from here to the hut-door."

"It doesn't look it," Cumshaw said promptly.

"It doesn't," his mate agreed. "But distance is deceptive here. How's the meal going?"

"Just about ready," Cumshaw told him. "I came to call you."

The two men walked side by side to the hut. At the entrance Cumshaw paused. "Nearer fourteen than ten," he said thoughtfully.

"Very likely," said Bradby indifferently. "What about that meal? I'm as hungry as a hunter."

They were on short commons. Bradby ate heartily, remarking once that there'd be food enough to go round to-morrow. Cumshaw laughed and said he hoped so, but that to-morrow was a day that never came to some people. Bradby absently ignored the challenge in Cumshaw's reply and kept silence for the rest of the time.

After breakfast the two of them took the saddle-bags down to the hole, placed them inside, and then stamped the earth tightly down on top of them.

"Now that's done," said Bradby, with an air of relief, "the sooner we get out of here the better."

"How about old bones over there?" Cumshaw said, pointing to the skeleton.

"Better sling him into the bushes," Bradby suggested, all his superstitious fears vanishing now that it was broad daylight.

"Poor old sinner," said Cumshaw as he lifted up the remains in his strong arms. "It might just as easily be one of us."

"Don't talk like that!" Bradby cried. "It's tempting Providence."

"You and I, Jack, have tempted that same all the days of our lives, and we're likely to keep on until the end, so why growl about this particular incident?"

Bradby muttered something unintelligible, and Cumshaw, who was all for haste now that their work was finished, did not ask him to repeat his remark.

Both horses had cropped their fill of grass, and the lame one seemed slightly better. Its limp was not so pronounced and the swelling had gone down.

"It's out of the question getting them out the way we got them in," Cumshaw said. "I wonder if there's any other way."

"Nothing like having a try," Bradby advised. "That darned old hermit must have come in some way, and I don't reckon it was the way we came in. If I was you I'd try over there towards the west. The hills look low enough."

So they turned off at right angles to their path and presently were edging their way through the wood again. As Bradby had surmised, the ground rose steadily, though it was very rough. Big boulders lay about the ground amongst the trees, which were thinning off. Soon they emerged on to what was open country, and speedily found themselves right under a ledge of rock which rose sheerly above their heads to a height of twenty or thirty feet.

"Blocked!" said Bradby savagely.

"No," said Cumshaw in a tone that implied he refused to acknowledge defeat. "There must be some way out, Jack, and I'm going to look until I find it. Here, you take charge of the horses and I'll fossick out something."

He was gone for ten minutes, ten long minutes that Bradby occupied in cursing the valley in particular and the rest of the world in general. Then there came a cry from the height above him, and, looking up, he saw Abel Cumshaw waving to him. Next instant the man disappeared and a few seconds later swung down through the rocks.

"It's no use," he said. "We can't take the horses out here. We'll just have to leave them. A man can crawl up through a sort of funnel in the wall of the rock, but you'd want a sling to get the horses along."

"Can't we go back and try the way we came in?"

Cumshaw shook his head decisively. "No," he said. "It won't do to risk it. They just tumbled down yesterday when we brought them, but you must remember that we had to cling on with our hands and feet when we went back. We'll have to jettison the horses."

"You said it was murder yesterday when I suggested shooting them," Bradby reminded him.

"We had a chance of saving them then," Cumshaw argued, "but now it's either them or us. If we turn them loose, the police'll find them sooner or later. If we shoot them, it's over and done with, and even if anyone does wander in here by accident he's not going to come this way. If we let them roam about the valley, they naturally go over to the other side where the grass is, and the first fool that blundered in would see them and begin to wonder how they got there. You never want to give the other man food for thought, Jack. Once he starts thinking, it's only a matter of time until he noses out everything."

"Shoot the horses, Abel, and have done with it. I'm sick and tired of talking. It's high time we did something."

The horses were shot then and there as the easiest way out of it, and when the echoes had died away the two men crawled cautiously up the funnel-like opening in the rock. Footholds were precarious enough, but by dint of hanging on by teeth and claw the partners at length forced their way to the top and stood on the ledge that overhung the valley. Across the smoky sea of timber they caught sight of the long line of golden wattle through which they had broken their way the previous evening. It occurred to both in almost the same instant that no man would be very likely to blunder in by chance. The place was securely hidden from view on three sides at least, and on the fourth, the side where they now stood, the approach was so difficult and, as they learnt later, dangerous that a man must have some very good reason for attempting it. Cumshaw it was who first put his thoughts into words.

"I can't help thinking," he said, "that the old chap must have come over from this side. Most likely he was dodging someone."

"I wouldn't be surprised at that," said the other.

"I don't think he'd have found the other way in a month of Sundays. However, let's get along. We'll have to make haste now we're without horses, What's it to be? Riverina or Adelaide?"

"I favor the Riverina," Cumshaw said. "I'm more familiar with the country, and they've got nothing against me up there."

"Riverina it is then," Bradby agreed with a laugh. "All places are the same to me. I've no more liking for one than for another."

So it came about that the valley faded away into the dim distance south of them, and presently they were toiling across the barrier of mountains that cuts Northern Victoria off from the rest of the State.

The tragedy happened that evening. An hour or so before

sunset they decided to camp hard by a little creek they had just discovered. Cumshaw, as usual, tended to the fire, and Bradby, after idling about for a while, suggested that he had better go hunting, in the hope of being able to obtain fresh meat for the meal.

"All right," said Cumshaw. "Go ahead. But don't be any longer than you can help."

"I'll be back as soon as I can," Bradby answered, and slipped into the shadows that were already gathering thick and fast. Abel Cumshaw worked away, whistling softly to himself the while. He was so busy doing one thing and another that it was not until darkness fell suddenly and completely on the scene that he realised how quickly time had passed. His first thought then was that Bradby was away much longer than he had any right to be. It occurred to him that Bradby might have gone much further than he intended and by some mischance had lost his way. He decided to wait a while longer, and then, if Bradby did not appear in the meantime, to go in search of him. But the time passed, the fire died away to red hot coals, and the shadows fell thickly on everything; but still Bradby did not come. At last Cumshaw rose swiftly to his feet in the manner of a man who has decided on the course he must take and means to stick to it unswervingly. With quick yet noiseless steps he stole through the trees, occasionally swinging a sharp glance to the left or right. But it was very dark in the woods, and it was impossible to tell shape from shadow. A regiment might have been hiding behind the boles of the trees without him being one whit the wiser. He had profound objections against shouting his whereabouts to his mate - his woods' instinct warned him never to reveal his presence unless there was no other way out - but he saw speedily enough that there was no other course left for him to take.

He made a megaphone of his hands, and sent a long-drawn "Coo-ee" out to wake the echoes. The sound reverberated from the hills and died rumbling away in the hollows. For some seconds after that there was absolute silence, and then somewhere ahead of him he caught a very faint noise as of long grass rustling in the wind. But the air was absolutely devoid of motion. The sound puzzled Cumshaw; the very stealthiness of it convinced him that no animal had made it, yet he could not understand why Bradby should exercise such unnecessary caution.

Then in an instant he knew. The black wall ahead of him was split by a pencil of flame, the silence of the forest crackled into sound, and the whip-like crack of a revolver echoed and re-echoed. A bullet whistled dangerously close to Cumshaw. He swore under his breath and tugged furiously at his own revolver. Bending almost double he sprinted towards the shelter of the nearest tree, while at the same instant the stranger's weapon cracked again. Something stung his ear. He put up his hand, and the warm blood spurted through his fingers.

He compressed himself into the smallest possible space behind the tree and then fired in the direction of the last shot. He allowed a short interval to elapse and then fired again. The other man must have seen the flashes, but he made no attempt to answer them. The moment the first shot was fired Cumshaw realised, in a flash of intuition, that his assailant was none other than Jack Bradby. The knowledge made him extremely angry, for such black treachery was the last thing he had expected to have to contend with. He saw now that it was the old case of thieves falling out over the division of the spoils, and that Jack Bradby was determined to stop at nothing, even murder, in order to gain the whole of the plunder. He continued firing with a savage fury that boded ill for his late mate.

The thing itself happened suddenly. One moment he was peering out into the darkness in an effort to locate his enemy; the next strong sinewy hands were around his throat choking the life out of him. With that clarity of vision that comes to a man perhaps once in a lifetime, he saw, even in the all-pervading darkness, the shadowy face that was pressed close to his own. The eyes that looked into his were dim pools of evil light, faintly phosphorescent like those of a cat, and the face that framed them was contorted into a malignant leer of triumph. That much he saw before the darkness crushed him out of existence and all things earthly faded from his vision.

Bradby felt the man's body go limp in his arms, and he quickly thrust into its holster the revolver with which he had dealt the final blow. There was a steamy smell of blood on the thick, damp air, and when Mr. Bradby drew away his right hand he found it warm and wet.

"Christ!" he said in a tone of fear, "I've killed him!" That was precisely what he had intended to do from the very first, but now his plan had apparently fructified, he felt a vague horror at the result of his handiwork. He opened Cumshaw's shirt and put his hand over the man's heart. He could not detect even the faintest flutter.

Then swiftly, with many glances about him as he moved, he carried the body to the undergrowth and very gently laid it on the ground. But he failed to notice that as he bent down a flat piece of wood had slipped from the pocket of his shirt and had fallen soundlessly into the soft green grass at the side of Abel Cumshaw's body.

Five minutes later silence reigned. Only the heavy scent of the wattle was mingled with another odor - the warm, sickly smell of freshly-shed blood.

CHAPTER V

EXPIATION

Unaccountably enough Bradby went no further than the dying embers of the fire. His first act was to build a big blaze, for he was already becoming afraid. He could not define even to himself just what this fear was; it was not so much horror at what he had done as a feeling that his sins would yet find him out. Some strange attraction kept him close to the scene of the tragedy, and all night he sat by the fire with his head in his hands and his eyes staring at the ever-widening ring of white ashes. Towards morning he fell into a doze, but scarcely had the first rays of the sun penetrated through the leafy mantle of the trees than he was wide-awake. There were dark rings under his eyes, and the eyes themselves looked strangely tired and haggard. He glanced at his hands with a faint idea that something had been wrong with them the night before. He was disgusted to find that they were caked with dried blood, and a feeling almost akin to nausea shook his frame. He made all the haste he could to the creek and washed every speck of blood and dirt off, so that when he had finished his hands were clean and spotless.

He shot a parrot for breakfast and made a gruesome meal off the raw flesh. There was nothing else to eat, for the flour had all been finished the previous day. After the morning's meal he brightened up and set off northward with a brisk stride. The money was safe enough in the valley for the present, he decided, and a couple of months in the Riverina would not only not do him any harm, but would allow the hue and cry time to die down. After that he would come back and get the gold, and this time there would be no question of division; it would be his, all of it. Now that the daylight had come he could think of the dark figure suddenly growing limp in his arms and the smell of fresh blood mixing with the scent of the wattles without the slightest misgiving. He had no fear of it; he certainly felt no remorse. The further he got from the scene of the murder, the lighter grew his spirits. He turned the situation over in his mind and found abundant satisfaction in it; his primitive logic told him that there was no evidence against him.

* * * * *

It is doubtful who was the most surprised, the troopers or Bradby when he stumbled unexpectedly into their camp that evening. They were not the men who had been following the bushrangers from the start, but another body, warned by wire and hurriedly sent out from Murtoa. For some unexplained reason the camp-fire had been allowed to die down, and so there was no red glow to warn Bradby of their proximity. He had blundered into the midst of the men before he quite realised what had happened, and, when he made a wild dash for safety, he found that all way of escape had been cut off. He was hemmed in on every side. The troop was in charge of an officer of more than average intelligence, and he instantly jumped to the correct conclusion. Had Bradby not lost his head and endeavored to escape, he might have been able to pass himself off as a prospector or something of the sort, but the mere sight of his all-too-evident anxiety to get away wakened the suspicions of the sergeant. The Grampians and the country surrounding them had hitherto been singularly free from crime, and no malefactors from other parts of the State were known to be at large in that neighbourhood. Obviously this man, who displayed such a disinclination to meet the police, must be a criminal, and just as obviously must he be one of the men wanted for the gold escort robbery. The sergeant decided in one lightning flash on a plan that he hoped would startle the man into betraying himself. The moment Bradby turned to retreat and found himself hemmed in, the other walked over to him, scrutinised him carefully, and in the same instant placed his hand on his shoulder and said, "I arrest you in the Queen's name for the robbery of the Gold Escort on the night of 1st December."

Bradby's jaw dropped and he stared open-mouthed at the other. He could not understand the process of almost instantaneous reasoning by which the officer had arrived at this conclusion, and the swift scrutiny the man had given him convinced him that in some strange and unaccountable way a description of him had been obtained and circulated. The man had recognised him, of that he felt sure.

All round him were staring policemen, watching him intently with eyes that were no less full of astonishment than his own. They could not fathom the reasons that actuated their chief, but they realised, all of them, that the man before them must be in some guilty way connected with the robbery. His very manner told them that.

The chief uttered the usual warning: "It is my duty to warn you that anything you say will be used in evidence - " He got so far when Bradby awoke from his stupor. He gave no warning of his intention, but his doubled fist shot out, caught the other on the point of the jaw and dropped him in a heap on the ground. Then with the swiftness of thought he leaped to one side, pulling his revolver loose at the same instant. He had just the smallest fraction of a second's start of the police, and in the flurry of the moment he actually burst through the cordon that had formed around him. The next instant the carbines of the police commenced to bark. Bradby stumbled, recovered himself, and fired over his shoulder. Several of the troopers were already on horseback, and it was only a matter of riding him down. He saw this himself, and his futile shot was designed to stop one at least of the horses. However, it went wide. He slipped behind a tree and began snap-shooting at the advancing mounted men. They spread out fanwise, thus coming at him from three sides at once. He moved slightly in order to get a better aim, and in doing so unwittingly exposed himself. One of the troopers, who had discarded his carbine in favor of a revolver, took a flying shot. Bradby lurched from behind the tree, clasped his hands to his left side and slipped down on to the grass.

When they reached him the blood was welling out of his side, and they saw that he was mortally wounded. The man who had fired the fatal shot dropped on his knees beside him and lifted up his head. Bradby's face was ashy pale, even in the faint moonlight one could see that, but he was still conscious.

"It's no use," he panted. "I'm done."

"Where is the gold and where are your mates?" the man asked, conscious that a word from the dying bushranger would solve everything. Bradby's frame shook spasmodically, and when the other looked again there was blood on his pale lips.

"Through the lung," muttered one of the others who had some knowledge of medical science.

The first man repeated his question in another form.

Bradby looked at him with a strangely inscrutable face and with eyes that were already darkening with the shadow of death.

"Where's the gold? Where's ... my ... mates?" The last three words were almost whispered.

"Yes," said the trooper eagerly. "Where are they?"

The dying man moved his lips, but no sound issued from them. The other bent down closer to him.

"That," said the bushranger with long and painful pauses between each word, "you ... will ... never ... know."

And with that last taunt on his lips he died.

"Game to the end," the trooper said to his comrades with an admiration he made no effort to hide.

* * * * *

The blow had not killed Abel Cumshaw. He lay unconscious for the better part of the night, and even when the day dawned he was too weak at first to do more than crawl a few paces at the most. His head was throbbing, his mouth was a raging furnace, and all his limbs felt as if they had been racked and twisted. When daylight came at length he lay still for a while, trying to recollect what had happened. But his mind was a perfect blank and he himself was a man without an identity. The blow that had knocked him unconscious had somehow affected his memory, and he knew no more about himself than he did about the man in the moon. Something terrible had happened, something in which he had played a very prominent part, that much he realised; but beyond that simple fact his recollection did not extend. He groped about in the grass in the hope that he might find something that would give him a clue to the situation. His hand fell on his revolver. That at least was tangible, but there was nothing enlightening about it. Further search revealed a small flat piece of wood. He picked it up curiously and stared at it. Two or three sentences had been hurriedly scratched on its smooth surface with the point of a sharp knife, but though they were intelligible enough they did not appear to refer to anything concerning him. The mere fact that he had been lying almost on top of the wood struck him as strange, and in a moment of unusual thoughtfulness he slipped it into his pocket.

It was bright day by then, and the warmth of the sun seemed to revive him to a marvellous extent. He got on his feet more by sheer will-power than by any sudden accession of strength. He found that he could stagger along, though his pace was necessarily slow and his course very erratic. Some uncharted sense, instinct perhaps, led him along the track to the creek where he had pitched his camp the previous evening. There was a dim familiarity about the place that puzzled him. He felt in some absurd way that he should recognise it, and he was both angry and surprised that he could not. He found the remains of the parrot that Bradby had eaten for breakfast, and he wondered vaguely who the man might be who had been so close to him that morning. His wonder was such an impersonal thing that he did not connect his own condition with the fact of the other man's presence. Something had given way inside his head, that something that controlled rational and consecutive memory. He sat down on the bank of the creek and gazed into space. It would be incorrect to say that he was dazed or that he behaved like a man in a dream. Those are stock terms that in themselves are quite inadequate to convey his peculiar state of mind and body. It was something more than lassitude, yet it was not quite fatigue. It was rather as if some integral part of his brain had been removed.

It is impossible to say just how long he remained on the bank of the creek. At last his hunger became so acute that he determined to go off foraging. He had his revolver with him; he was a fair enough shot, and so it was not long before he tumbled a 'possum out of a tree. He made a rough meal of it, and after that set off aimlessly into the bush. Had he kept to his original intention he would have speedily wandered into the Mallee, and would have run a good chance of dying of starvation in that thinly-populated district. But his mind was still in a whirl, and instinct alone guided his footsteps to the east. He was many miles north of the valley and during his travels he moved further north, so that he did not come across it during his journey back.

His subsequent adventures are not very clear. Early in his travels the piece of wood began to trouble him, and he decided that the sooner he got rid of it the better. It is more than likely that he connected it in some way with that blank feeling of inexplicable tragedy which seemed to overshadow him. His instinct, however, led him to hide rather than destroy it. He read the wording very carefully, but it failed to awaken any responsive chords in his memory. As an after-thought, just as he was about to slide the wood into the hole he had scraped out, he took his knife and cut his name below the screed. Then he thrust it into the hole and stamped the earth in on top of it. In this relation it is interesting to notice the connection between the hiding of the money and the burying of the wood that held the key to the position of the former. It seems as if the sub-conscious memory of the one act had its influence on the man in his performance of the other.

Thereafter Mr. Cumshaw simply disappeared off the face of the earth. His son's story is that he went to New South Wales, married there and raised a family, and in the light of subsequent events that seems to be what most likely occurred. It is known, however, that the Cumshaws were in Victoria again somewhere about nineteen hundred and two or three, Albert being at that time seven years old.

With the lapse of years Abel had gradually recovered his memory, and bit by bit most of the incidents of the robbery had stolen out of the shrouded darkness of the past. He appears to have been perfectly contented with his family, and for one reason and another the gold remained undisturbed through the long years. The time was coming when the old play would be staged again and new actors would arise to carry it through.

The tale of the gold robbery and the shooting of Mr. Jack Bradby, as the reader will readily understand, passed into the police records and thus became matters of history. Though no definite statement has been left us, Mr. Bryce must have first come across the story during his researches into Victorian history. He had friends in the Department, and it is quite feasible that he had ready access to many official documents that are usually beyond the reach of the ordinary public. He was not the only one in this enviable position. There were other students of the past who were moving along the same lines, and as he pieced together the puzzle of the robbery he was followed by a pair of agile, unscrupulous brains every whit as clever as he. The police records told Mr. Bryce just this much: - On the first day of December, 1881, there had been a gold robbery, and the robbers had got completely away. They had been followed, and subsequently a man had been killed in the Grampians who had been identified as John Bradby, a noted sheep and cattle-duffer. When dying he refused to tell who his pals were, and had in the same breath stated that the police would never find the gold. That in itself was conclusive, yet the additional fact remained that the whereabouts of the gold was still as big a mystery as ever it had been. The opinion of the police was that the other members of the gang - they seemed to think that it was a fairly large one - had returned when the hue and cry had died away and recovered the plunder. Bryce, reading between the lines of the dry official record, rather thought that they hadn't. At any rate the element of mystery was sufficiently strong to induce him to investigate the matter further. That was really the beginning of the trouble.

CHAPTER VI

THE HEGIRA OF MR. ABEL CUMSHAW

Early in January, 1919, Mr. Bryce had advanced so far in his investigations that he resolved on taking a trip to the country around the Grampians. He had nothing very definite to go on beyond the facts that the robbery had been committed at one spot and Mr. Bradby had been killed at another, and logically the gold must have been hidden somewhere in between. He had hopes that he might stumble on something that in his capable hands would prove to be a clue to the long-lost hiding-place of the gold. Before he made any preparations he inserted an advertisement in several of the leading dailies. It ran somehow like this: - "Wanted - A capable and intelligent assistant to take part in dangerous expedition to Grampians. Apply," and then followed his name and address. He was convinced in his own mind that someone amongst those who read this notice would have some inkling at least of the events of 1st December, 1881, and he rather fancied that he or they would be on the alert. In that case it was just possible that the persons concerned would either approach him with a guarded offer or would dog his footsteps. In either case there was a chance of Mr. Bryce picking up information that might be to his immediate advantage. He convinced himself that there were still people living who had played an intimate part in the affairs of that memorable night.

The advertisement, however, had two results that were unforeseen by Mr. Bryce. The third day after the insertion of the notice he was informed that a gentleman wanted to see him. He requested that the man be shown into his study. In due course the visitor arrived. He was a man somewhere in the neighbourhood of sixty, but, save for a slight greying of the hair about his temples, he showed little outward signs of his age. His eyes, which were of a deep, unfathomable black, were very alert and followed Mr. Bryce's every movement with a glittering serenity, if one can use the expression, that was very disturbing.

"Sit down," said Mr. Bryce, and he waved his visitor to a chair.

The man sat down in the chair indicated, looked Mr. Bryce up and down, without, however, the least sign of offensiveness in his gaze, and said without any further preliminary, "I've come to see you about that advertisement."

"Um!" said Mr. Bryce non-committally. "Yes, that ad. What about it?"

"I think," said the other with his eyes fixed intently on Mr. Bryce, "I think I am the best man for the job."

"I haven't told you yet what the job is," Mr. Bryce objected.

"That's so," the other admitted. "Beyond saying that it was dangerous, you did not attempt to describe it. It doesn't matter what you want in the Grampians. I'm the man to take. I know the place well."

"It's changed vastly in thirty years," Bryce said suddenly.

The other must have been expecting something like this, for he never turned a hair. As far as he was concerned Mr. Bryce's observation might have been the most casual remark in the world. He ignored it. Perhaps it would have been better had he commented on it and asked what association to-day's expedition had with what had happened during thirty odd years. He passed the matter over in silence, and in that instant

Bryce guessed that the man knew as much, if not more, than he did.

"Do you know why I advertised that expedition as dangerous?" Bryce asked, seeing that the other made no attempt to reply.

The man shook his head. "No, I don't," he said distinctly.

"I'll tell you," said Bryce, and he leaned forward in simulated confidence. "I'm fat and I wheeze. My bellows are all to blazes and the doctors won't give a rap for my heart. I might go out any minute, more especially if there's any extra exertion. Now I want a man who won't ask questions, who will do the exertions for two, and take what's coming with a grin."

"That sounds simple enough," the man remarked. "May I ask what we are after?"

"I'm searching for gold," said Bryce with a startling clearness.

The other shifted in his seat, looked at Bryce as if to measure the possibilities of his next remark, and then said, "There's no gold there."

"You mean," said Bryce, "that none's ever been discovered there; quite a different thing. I hope to discover some before I'm done."

"It's too far west for mines," the other asserted.

Mr. Bryce passed over the man's statement in a way that showed that as far as he was concerned that aspect of the matter was over and done with. The obvious answer for him to make would have been, "Gold comes in other ways than out of mines," but he was cautious enough not to air all his knowledge at once.

"What's your name?" he demanded.

"Abel Cumshaw," the other answered, and saw by the way Bryce screwed up his brows that it conveyed nothing to him.

"Well, Mr. Cumshaw, would you care to take this job on?"

"How long would we be away?"

"Six weeks or two months. I'm not certain of that."

"When do we start?"

"This is Monday. Be here Friday and we'll get right away. Friday morning, mind, at ten-thirty sharp. That's all, I think. Good-day."

After Mr. Cumshaw had gone Bryce slipped back in his chair and laughed till his whole face creased up in rolls of quivering fat. "That's a good one on him," he murmured. "He didn't ask what screw he was to get, and I didn't tell him because I wanted to see if he'd ask. But he didn't, so he must have been thinking of something else. He's anxious to get to the Grampians, darned anxious. From the way he went on he seems to know a bit about the place too. I wonder has he any suspicion?... Good Lord! wouldn't it be a streak of luck if he knew! Yes, I did the right thing in sending in that ad. One man's bitten at any rate."

He went about the house all day chuckling away to himself.

* * * * *

The second incident which occurred that same day was of even a more disturbing nature. Late that afternoon the telephone bell rang, and when Bryce answered it a voice asked if he was the Mr. Bryce who had advertised for an assistant in an expedition to the Grampians.

"That's me," said Bryce. "But I'm sorry to say that the position's filled."

"Why are you sorry?" the voice asked disconcertingly.

"Um!" said Mr. Bryce. "Aren't you after it?"

"No chance," said the voice. "As a matter of fact, I was on the point of writing out a similar one myself, when I saw yours and guessed I'd let you do the work."

"Who are you?" Bryce demanded with a trace of sharpness in his voice.

The man at the other end of the wire laughed cheerfully. "Never you mind," he said. "You'll know soon enough, as soon as you've landed Jack Bradby's plunder. Now, I want to put up a sporting proposition to you. We'll retire gracefully, if you'll split fifty-fifty."

"We!" Bryce repeated. "So there's more than one of you?"

"There's lots of us, and we've got the whip hand of you because, you see, you don't know who we are. We know you; we've been following a couple of jumps behind you right through all the records, and we guess it's high time we cashed in."

"I'll see you in Hell first!" said Bryce angrily.

"Probably you will," said the voice with a chuckle. "If you won't treat with us, we'll get what we want in other ways."

"No, by thunder, you won't!" said Bryce shortly. "I'll warn you that I'll shoot on sight."

"So do we," the other laughed. "I hope, for your sake, you recognise us first, though I don't think it likely."

"If I catch you monkeying around I'll fill you so full of holes that your own mother won't know you from a colander," Bryce threatened; but the voice laughed irritatingly, and when

Bryce tried to get a reply he found that the other had rung off.

He flickered the hook with his finger. "Exchange," he said, giving his number, "can you tell me who was speaking just now?"

"Box three, G. P. O. public 'phones," said the girl wearily.

"Oh, hell!" said Bryce in disgust, and hung up the receiver.

* * * * *

The rest of the week passed without incident of any sort, and, despite the warning he had received. Bryce went on calmly with his preparations. For all the fat flabbiness of him he was grit through and through, and it took more than a warning over the telephone to turn him aside once he had made up his mind to take a certain course. He went on quietly and silently; his only sign of perturbation was that first thing on Tuesday he slipped down town and bought a big calibre revolver.

Friday morning came, and at ten-thirty exactly, not a minute before or after, Mr. Abel Cumshaw knocked at the front door and was admitted. He was shown at once into Mr. Bryce's study, where that gentleman awaited him, watch in hand.

"On time to the tick," he said affably as Cumshaw entered the room. "Everything's ready for an immediate start. I suppose you've got all you want."

"I'm always ready at a moment's notice," Cumshaw said. "I travel light. I'm an old campaigner."

"That's the way I like to hear a man talk," Bryce said breezily. "We'll be going in my car as far as we can. After that we'll have to walk, and I'm not a very good hand at that. There's some rough spots up there, they tell me," he said off-handedly. For all his seeming nonchalance he was watching Cumshaw intently, and he saw him give an almost imperceptible start. It flashed across Bryce's mind that perhaps Cumshaw was in the pay of the people who had gone to such pains to 'phone him. A second look at the man convinced him that such was not the case. Cumshaw's eyes were frank and clear, and met his unswervingly. They were not the eyes of a man who was playing a double game.

There was something in them that Bryce did not quite understand. It was the animation of newly-resurrected hope, such a light as might have shone in the eyes of the men who rode to find the Holy Grail. Bryce knew nothing of him or his history, and his only thought was that in some queer way the man had a vital interest in the Grampians. It must be remembered that, as far as known facts were concerned, Bryce knew nothing more than the police records had told him. True, his reasoning faculties, which were none of the densest, carried him a little further, but he would have been the very first to admit his fallibility. Nothing had occurred as yet to connect Cumshaw with Mr. Jack Bradby. He recognised that the man had a definite object in view in going to the Grampians - that was plain enough - but it might after all be merely coincidence. Such things have happened. Mr. Cumshaw, on the other hand, was alert and suspicious. He suspected everybody and everything, and he had answered the advertisement solely because he believed, or affected to believe, that an expedition to the hill country could have no other object that the recovery of the gold. Doubtless it will appear strange that Mr. Cumshaw had allowed so many years to elapse without attempting to secure it for himself, but, as he told Bryce later on, there were reasons even for that.

* * * * *

They stopped at Ballarat for lunch; Bryce refilled the petrol tank, and then they set out on the long stretch to Ararat. Though no definite statement exists, they passed the night at the latter town, for Cumshaw afterwards told his son that they reached Landsborough about 10.30 the following morning. Beyond Landsborough the track became very trying for the car, and somewhere towards the evening of the second day the machine was hidden away securely in one of the many gullies that abounded in the neighbourhood. Then the hardest part of the journey began. Child's play though it might have been to Cumshaw, who, for all his years, had a constitution such as it is given to a few men to possess, it certainly must have been a matter of infinite torture to Bryce, handicapped as he was with his weak-heart and his wheezy lungs.

They spent the next few days in working across to the spot where Bradby had been killed thirty odd years before. As they drew near to the place Cumshaw became more self-contained and uncommunicative than ever. The sight of the old scene seemed to have depressed him marvellously. Bryce watched him with increasing attentiveness; he noticed that he picked out the road as if he had been used to it from childhood. There were times when Bryce turned suddenly on him and caught a glimpse of a hard-set jaw and a mouth about which strong lines of determination had woven themselves. Yet, as soon as Cumshaw fancied he was observed, the mask of his face melted into a smile, and the sombre eyes sparkled with a humor that somehow seemed too real to be assumed.

"You seem very familiar with the place, Cumshaw," Bryce remarked one morning.

"I told you I was," Cumshaw answered, his unfathomable eyes searching his employer's face.

"How long is it since you were here last?" Bryce asked.

At the question all expression vanished from the other's face, leaving it as immobile as a carven image of stone. "I have been here many times," he said evasively.

"Um!" said Bryce in that peculiar way of his, and he looked the other up and down contemplatively. "I didn't think anyone had been here since Bradby was shot."

Bryce made the remark in the most casual and innocent way; he hadn't the faintest notion in the world that what he had said was like a bombshell bursting beneath the structure of Mr. Cumshaw's composure. He was intelligent enough to realise that it was more than probable that Cumshaw possessed knowledge of that almost forgotten episode which was not shared with anyone else, but he had not the least suspicion that his casual utterance would hit home so shrewdly as it did.

Mr. Cumshaw stared at him as if he could not believe his ears. For once he made no attempt to disguise his emotions beneath the mask of stoicism. He saw laughter in the other's eyes, the jovial laughter of a man who has always known the sweets of victory, and he jumped to the natural though erroneous conclusion that Bryce had fathomed his connection with the late Mr. Bradby. For all that he did not abandon his defences without some show of resistance.

"What do you mean?" he demanded in the belligerent attitude of a man who is fighting a desperate though losing fight.

"Just what I said, Mr. Cumshaw," Bryce smiled. "What else did you think I meant?"

The quiet question was put in such an unexpectedly mild tone that Cumshaw was left wordless for the nonce, though his face showed in all their fulness the emotions that were stirring within him. Doubt, indecision, fear of a kind.

"I thought - ," he said and then stopped short.

"You thought," Bryce repeated with a gentle persuasiveness in his voice. "What was it you thought, Cumshaw?"

They were both fencing, in sporting parlance "sparring for wind," each of them with the Big Idea almost within reach, and each not daring yet to put it into words. For the space of a heart-beat they stared into each other's eyes, seeking to read the other's thoughts. In the end it was Cumshaw who gave in first. He tore his eyes away from that fixed yet kindly gaze that seemed to search and read his very soul.

"I see," said Bryce, with a sudden intake of breath that lent a sibilant quality to his speech, "I see that we are on the same track. Mr. Cumshaw, place your cards on the table. You are after the gold that Bradby hid; so am I. Our aims are the same. Let us be partners, instead of employer and assistant. What do you know that I do not? What do I know that you do not?"

Like most fat and comfortable people Bryce was the soul of generosity, and his offer was dictated not so much by expediency as by a sense of the pity that he felt for this man, who seemed to have aged years in the last few minutes. He, too, in his time had known what it meant to have the prize within a hand's touch and then at the last moment lose it after all.

"You know nothing about me," Cumshaw said impulsively. "You don't know who I am or what I've been. You haven't an idea...."

Bryce cut him short with a sweeping gesture of his chubby hands. "My dear man," he said, "what you've been doesn't matter a tinker's curse to me. It's what you are that counts."

"You don't even know that," the other answered, his lips curling in a wry smile.

"I'll know as soon as you tell me," Bryce hinted.

It is a difficult matter for a man, who all his life has held a close secret, to divulge it at a moment's notice, in a sudden fit of warm friendliness, to a comparative stranger, and so Abel Cumshaw found it. It is even harder to surrender one's hopes and ambitions in favor of a potential rival, honest and all as that rival may appear to be. For one brief moment Cumshaw paused on the brink of revelation, the while he weighed the matter in his mind. In some strange way Bryce had guessed that he was after the gold, but did he know why and how? Cumshaw rather fancied he didn't. He was so sure of it that he decided that he would gain nothing by divulging the connection between himself and the late Mr. Bradby. So the mouth which was opening to speak shut up again like a steel trap, and the dark eyes turned bleak and cold. He looked Bryce steadily and calmly in the face.

"There is nothing to tell," he said, and turned on his heel.

* * * * *

Black night had descended on the forest many hours before, so many in fact that the camp fire had sunk to a feeble red glow, and the dying embers were already circled by a ring of dead white ash. The breeze was crooning softly through the branches of the trees, singing weird chanties to itself. In between the murmurs of the wind there came another sound, the indistinct sound of a sleepy man mumbling to himself. Bryce half-raised himself on one elbow and listened. Half a dozen feet away from him Cumshaw lay tightly rolled in his blankets. He tossed restlessly and once all but sat up. Bryce dropped quickly but soundlessly back into a prone position. But the alarm had been a false one, and presently he quietly raised himself again. The indistinct mumbling went on as before, and he strained his ears to catch some intelligible word.

"Kill me, would you?" he heard the other say.

His voice sank again, and for a time he mumbled and mouthed his words so that Bryce missed most of what he said. He was just on the point of settling down again when Cumshaw suddenly sat up.

"I'll beat you yet, Bradby!" he cried with startling distinctness. "You're dead now and the gold's mine."

His eyes opened and he stared dazedly around him. Bryce was lying prone and snoring away hoggishly. He was fast asleep;

there was not the slightest doubt in the mind of the man who watched him so closely.

"I must have dreamt I said it," Cumshaw murmured to himself. "If I'd spoken the way I thought I had he'd have been wide-awake." And then he in his turn composed himself to slumber.

* * * * *

They were very quiet at breakfast. Bryce was turning the situation over in his mind, viewing it from all possible angles and seeking some method of getting Cumshaw to speak without in any way antagonising him. Cumshaw himself was troubled by lingering doubts. It was quite possible after all that Bryce had heard him, supposing he had spoken aloud, and was quietly dissembling for some purpose of his own. His very thoughtfulness seemed to lend color to that idea. He looked at Bryce across the carpet of grass and at the same instant Bryce raised his eyes. They stared at each other with the breathless intensity of two men who know that in all things they are evenly matched. Each was striving to the last atom of his will-power to break down the resistance of the other and force him in some way to take the initiative. At last it was Bryce who dropped his eyes a fraction and Cumshaw who breathed a sigh of relief. But his relief was short-lived, for in the last half-second his guard had relaxed. Bryce said:

"Why did Bradby want to kill you, Mr. Cumshaw?"

The quick yet calm question, covering as it did the one episode of which nobody but the two participants could possibly have any knowledge, startled Cumshaw. For once his impassive face showed signs of fear, and his eyes became those of a hunted man. He half-rose to his feet and then dropped back again, as if aware of the uselessness of flight. He tried to speak, but the words stuck in his throat. In one short sentence Bryce had shattered all his hopes and pulled his airy castles to the ground. Did this man but like to speak he would be once again

Cumshaw the bushranger, the man who had been hand in glove with Bradby, and who, through some miracle of mischance, had not been bracketed with his dead colleague. Bryce knew all apparently, and a word from him - . Cumshaw shivered.

"You can trust me," Bryce said softly. "I guess I know your secret now. You and Bradby carried out that robbery between you. You hid the gold, and for one reason and another you've never retrieved it. Isn't that it?"

Cumshaw nodded. It was too late now to deny anything, even if he had so felt inclined. Nemesis in the shape of this laughing-eyed, gross-bodied man, had come upon him in his old age, and there was nothing for it but to take what was coming with as good a grace as he could muster.

"What happened thirty years or more ago is over and done with," Bryce ran on, "and I'm not the sort to bring it into the light of day again. I'm after that gold, and, in order to get it, I'm quite ready to repeat my previous offer. We each seem to have something that the other lacks. You can tell me many things I don't know. Of that I'm sure."

"There's a lot of things you seem sure of," Cumshaw said with a half-defiant air.

"I'm as sure that you're the man who was with Bradby as if I'd seen it all myself," Bryce stated. "Remember, before you refuse, that it's always better to compromise than fight. Furthermore, if you have to fight, it's much better to have an ally you can rely on."

"What's that?" Cumshaw demanded with a show of interest. "What do you mean?"

"Only this," Bryce said slowly. "There's another crowd on the track, and they've already warned me that they'll make the going heavy. If you've got to be up against them, why not throw in your lot with me? It's fifty-fifty with us; if you stand out on your own, you'll probably lose it all."

"I think you've got me in a cleft stick," Cumshaw said a trifle ruefully. "I can't see that I can refuse. Now how much do you know?"

Said Mr. Bryce untruthfully, "I know everything except where you've hidden the gold."

"And even I couldn't swear to that," Cumshaw said.

"It seems to me," said Bryce dryly, "that the best thing you can do is to tell me the whole story."

He listened eagerly to the tale, occasionally stopping the other to question him on some obscure point, sometimes helping him along with a comment that threw unexpected light in the dark corners of the story.

"It amounts to this," he said when Cumshaw had finished. "Bradby buried the gold in this hidden valley of yours. It's so hidden - the valley, I mean - that you only came on it by accident, and you have no definite idea as to its whereabouts. It's three or four days' journey into the mountains, that's all you can say. There's no way of recognising it from the outside that you know of. Well, I'll tell you this, Mr. Cumshaw. It's my frank opinion that your clever murderous friend had some way of finding it again, or he wouldn't have been in such haste to make away with you. He knew what he was doing, you can depend on it. Now I wonder if he left any clue?"

"I've got a hazy memory that he left directions somewhere and that I had them," Cumshaw said despondently, "but I can't say what happened to them. You must remember that I was wandering about half-delirious for a long while after I got knocked, and it was years before I got really right again. I might have lost any note he made; I might have done anything with it."

"You might have and that's a fact," Mr. Bryce agreed. "Now you say you've hunted for this valley many times during the last ten years or so."

Cumshaw nodded. "It seems funny," he said, "but I've never been able to find it."

"There's nothing funny about it," Bryce told him. "History and fiction abound with instances of similar miscalculations. I'll guarantee that there are scores of such places in every continent in the world. Australia's got just as many as any other place. What made you want to hunt it up again after all those years?"

"Old associations, I suppose," Cumshaw said half-ashamedly. "While I was in New South Wales - I went there, you understand, until things blew over a bit - and my wife was alive, I didn't want anything else but to be near her. When she died and things began to go wrong with me, I drifted back here. Money was short. I was living as best I could, and there were the children to look after, and the sight of the old places brought things back to my mind. I was beginning to dig bits up from the memory of the past - the doctors have some fancy name for lapses like mine, though I could never remember what it was - and then one day I asked myself why shouldn't I go after the gold? It was as much mine as anyone else's, now that Bradby was dead, and the Bank that originally owned it had gone smash about the Land Boom time from what I could gather. I went, but I missed the place somehow. I went time and again, but it was always like that 'Lost Mountain' story of Mayne Reid's, though a valley's harder to find than a mountain you'd think. I couldn't find it anyhow, and that's about all there is to it."

"Um!" said Mr. Bryce, and he ran his hand softly across his chin. "We are up against a bigger thing than I thought. I'm hanged if I can see a glimmer of light anywhere. Is there anything you can suggest?"

Cumshaw did not reply. He was staring straight ahead of him, staring intently, and little furrows of anxiety marred the serenity of his forehead. He was peering into the shadows of the trees as if his eyes were twin searchlights that could cut substance from the gloom. He was staring so intently that Bryce whirled round, fully convinced that his friends of the telephone were upon them.

"What's wrong?" he queried in a hoarse whisper. "What are you looking at?"

"Nothing," said Cumshaw. "I thought I heard something moving, that's all."

Bryce in his turn peered intently in between the tree-boles, but the shadows lay thick upon the grass between, and it was difficult to define even the shapes of the more distant timber. The place was still and gloomy, full of grim forebodings, like a summer sky in which a storm is gathering.

"We must have been mistaken," Bryce remarked in his embracing way. "There doesn't seem to be anyone about."

"Hands up!" snapped a crisp voice, and in the surprise of the moment Bryce obeyed. Cumshaw had no such intention. He dropped suddenly on to the ground even as a shot rang out, and a bullet whistled close above his head. The next instant he was crashing swiftly through the bushes, spinning down into the gully like a human projectile.

CHAPTER VIII

THE GATHERING OF THE EAGLES

At first Bryce could see nothing but the dull gleam of unpolished metal from the barrel of a revolver which protruded from behind a tree, but a further scrutiny showed him the dim outlines of a man's figure standing in that place of gloom and ghosts. The man stepped out from his hiding-place, even as Bryce watched him, and was followed almost instantly by another man. They were both somewhere about the same height, in the neighbourhood of five feet ten. Their features were not visible, for each of them wore a handkerchief about his face in the time-honored fashion of the men of the road, and a hat pulled well down over the eyes completed the disguise.

"Well, Mr. Bryce," said the man in front, "what have you got to say for yourself?"

"It's a funny thing," remarked Bryce, with the adventures of Mr. Cumshaw and the late Mr. Bradby in his mind, "it's funny how history repeats itself."

The leader made a step forward and stared intently at Bryce. "You're the man right enough," he said. "Where's your pal?"

"Ask me something easy," sneered Bryce, "and I'd be obliged if you'd let me drop my hands awhile. This is getting fairly tiresome."

"You should have thought of that before you started that business," the other one reminded him. "It's rather late now to be finding out the flaws in your plans."

The sneering smile on Mr. Bryce's face broadened into a grin of triumph. "Didn't you ever hear the proverb about glass-houses and the people who live in them?" he enquired blandly.

The first speaker stared at him, but the other one said impatiently, "Finish him off, Alick, and let's get it over."

The man called Alick answered in a subdued voice. Bryce did not catch what he said, but supposed it to be a counsel of caution. His smile grew in intensity, so much so that Alick snapped at him. "What the deuce are you grinning at, you fat fool?" he demanded.

"You'll know soon enough," Bryce said with a chuckle. He looked right past them into the shadows of the trees, on his face the joyful expression of a man who sees the long-locked gates of his prison swing open before him. Both men whirled round with a chorus of oaths. They were quite positive that Bryce's mate had stolen a march on them and crept up behind their backs. They had their heads turned away but for the fraction of a second, but the time, short though it was, was plenty long enough for Mr. Bryce. With an agility, remarkable in a man of his weight and state of health, he faded into the landscape like some fat fairy.

"Fooled!" said Alick's companion, and he whipped round to face his prisoner, only to find that the keen-brained Mr. Bryce had vanished as completely as if he had been blown off the face of the earth.

"Nice pair of goats we are," remarked Alick disgustedly.

The other said nothing, but stood for a moment in a state of indecision. At that precise instant a pencil of flame shot out from one of the trees immediately in front of them, and Alick dropped his revolver with a howl of pain.

"He's winged me," he said, and applied to Mr. Bryce an epithet not usually heard in polite society.

His mate fired at the tree from which the shot had evidently come, but the bullet did nothing more than flatten itself against the trunk in a shower of dust and dry bark. Mr. Bryce's revolver spoke once again. This time he failed to register.

"The sooner we get out of this the better," said Alick, with one hand clasped to his injured shoulder. "The beggar'll riddle us both if we stop here."

The other man grunted his approval of the suggestion and proceeded to carry it into effect at once.

"Better look where you are going," Alick advised. "That other chap's about somewhere, perhaps waiting for us."

The other consigned both Bryce and his assistant to a place more noted for its warmth than its comfort. Despite their forebodings Mr. Cumshaw did not put in an appearance, and they gained the shelter of the thick timber in safety.

Once he was sure that they had really departed Mr. Bryce stepped out from behind his tree, first, however, with commendable caution reloading the heavy revolver he carried. The smile was still flickering about the corners of his mouth, but there was a little wrinkle of anxiety across his forehead.

"I wonder where the devil Cumshaw's gone?" he remarked to the unresponsive trees. "He went off like a scared rabbit. I'd better hunt for him. I can't get on without him now."

With the laudable intention of finding Mr. Cumshaw as soon as possible he began to scour the neighbourhood.

When Mr. Cumshaw disappeared so precipitately it was with

the idea that he must maintain his freedom at any cost. True, Bryce might be captured, but by the same token he could be rescued just as easily. Though his intentions were right enough he was prevented in the simplest manner possible from carrying them into effect. He went crashing through the bushes as has already been related, and found himself on the edge of what was nothing more or less than a blind creek. The sides were covered with matted brushwood and were as slippery as glass. His momentum was such that he could not stop himself in time, and he went head over heels down the side of the gully, and spun on to the boulder-covered bottom like some new and monstrous kind of Catherine wheel. He collided with the rounded surface of one of the big weather-worn rocks which lay strewn about the gully floor like the tremendous marbles of a giant.

The world spun round him in a blaze of colored lights, and his head felt as if it were filled with fireworks. Then in an instant all sensation ceased as though cut off with the clean sweep of a naked sword. Mr. Cumshaw lay still and lifeless under the shadow of the brushwood-covered gully.

Some half an hour later, when Bryce happened on this very spot, he pulled the bushes aside cautiously and peered down almost between his toes; but the shadows lay thick beneath him, and the edge of the gully so projected that he could not see the body of the man for whom he was searching. Slowly he retraced his steps. He was deeply puzzled by this new aspect of the affair. It seemed impossible that Cumshaw could have completely disappeared in so short a space of time, yet the fact that he could not be found was in itself proof conclusive. Had Bryce lingered a couple of seconds longer he would have seen the rapidly-recovering Cumshaw turn over on his side, raise one hand to his head, and present a startled face to the scanty rays of light that filtered down to him. In a sense his revival was something more than a recovery; it was a resurrection. The years rolled away in an instant, and he ceased to be the Abel Cumshaw who had fallen down the side of the gully and cracked his head against an extra-large sized boulder; he became the Abel Cumshaw who had just been knocked into unconsciousness by the butt of Mr. Bradby's revolver, and whose head still throbbed with the force of the blow.

He stared uncomprehendingly at the steep sides of the gully; they had no place in his gallery of mental pictures. He had a vague idea that there should be a creek somewhere close at hand. His head was throbbing, pulsing as if some mighty engine were working inside it. He rose unsteadily to his feet and regarded the steep declivities which formed the sides of the gully with a contemplative eye. He decided that they were climbable, but that he must wait awhile before he made the attempt. He was weak yet; one does not recover instantaneously from a crack on the head. He moved very carefully when he moved at all, and he kept well within the shadows of the overhanging banks. Mr. Bradby was somewhere handy, he argued, extremely ready and willing to finish him off, and it would never do to give him another chance. He had no idea that Mr. Bradby had died long years ago. Time had telescoped and he was back again in the early eighties. With the addled craftiness of a half-witted creature he set about escaping from the imprisoning walls of the gully-dungeon. Had it been anything else than a blind creek he would have found an exit by following the dry bed, and thus have disappeared entirely from this story. But it was fated otherwise. The one idea that gained any sort of prominence in his mind was that he must climb the side of the gully.

He found a pool of clear rainwater in a little cavity in the dry bed of the creek, and bathed his head in it and drank a little. Its refreshing coolness acted on his jaded body like the sting of a spur on the flank of a lazy horse. He crept cautiously in under the overhang of the bank and searched about for a foothold. Such was not hard to find, and, in less time than it takes to write of it, he was swinging up the side of the bank, clinging to projecting ledges of rock with hands and feet that seemed to possess all the prehensile quality of a monkey's. Once on the top of the bank he burrowed into the mass of vegetation like some primeval creature taking to earth, a pitiful caricature of the sane, strong man he had been a few short hours before. Cautious and all as he was, his flight was not absolutely noiseless, and so it came about that presently Bryce heard him, and circled round the spot from which the sound came like a wolf heading off a herd of deer.

Cumshaw crashed through the bushes and emerged into the open a hundred yards or so ahead of Bryce. The latter caught sight of him at the moment of his emergence and called out to him to stop.

"Cumshaw," he called. "Come here!"

The other heard the call and caught his own name, but instead of slackening he accelerated his pace. He did not look round; he was convinced in his own warped mind that his pursuer was none other than the late Mr. Bradby. Accordingly he swung along at such a rate that Bryce soon dropped behind, breathless and dispirited. He sat down on a convenient log and mopped his damp face with a large-sized handkerchief. Presently his breathing became normal again, and his agitated heart ceased fluttering like a caged bird. He fell to reviewing the position. The more he thought of it, the less hopeless it appeared to be. His unrecognisable and nameless antagonists had temporarily withdrawn from the fight, whether to consolidate their forces and plan some new form of attack, or because they had received a very salutary lesson, he could not say. Also it did not worry him over much. His ideas were centred mainly on Mr. Cumshaw. True, that gentleman had disappeared over the horizon with every mark of unseemly haste, and already he must be well advanced on whatever road he was taking. Not so very far away the car awaited Bryce, and he was sure that, once he reached it, it would be merely a matter of a day or so until he rediscovered Mr. Cumshaw. He repeated the verb. "Rediscovered" struck a distinctive note. One could not convey the same meaning with any form of the verb "to overtake;" Mr. Cumshaw had disappeared, not simply gone on ahead. He chuckled softly at his own quaint conceit, and at that his spirits began to rise again.

Feeling now fully rested, he rose to his feet and swung out on the track with that long slow stride which was all that remained of his athletic form of the old New Guinea days. Of late years he had walked, when he had walked at all, with the quick nervous step of the city-bred man, and it heartened him immensely to know that he was recovering without any effort of his volition the old easy pioneer stride.

It is not within the scope of this tale to relate how Mr. Bryce at length reached his car and set out on what he believed to be Abel Cumshaw's trail. Suffice it to state that he reached his machine without any untoward incident, the two gentlemen who had so rudely disturbed the serenity of his nature having seemingly disappeared from the face of the earth. Once he passed a drover and elicited from him that a man answering Cumshaw's description had passed him on the road the previous morning. Evidently then the missing man was keeping away from the towns, taking instead a trail that would inevitably lead him further into the bush. He was rather pleased at this. Abel Cumshaw in the city would be as hard to find as the proverbial needle in a bundle of hay, but in the bush it would be much easier to locate him, Bryce considered. So he drove the car along at a low speed, keeping all the time a watchful eye out for any signs of the truant. As he progressed he was surprised and not a little pleased to find that his New Guinea woodcraft was coming back to him by degrees. The joy of the chase was his, and he experienced again the same keen and primitive emotions that had thrilled him in the days when the elder Carstairs and he had trodden the unexplored wilds of Papua.

* * * * *

He came upon Cumshaw very suddenly. The car was creeping through the trees at a snail's pace - there was no clearly defined track in that part of the bush, and Bryce was taking no unnecessary risks - when he caught sight of a figure that might or might not be the missing Mr. Cumshaw. He stopped the car at once and descended to the ground. As has already been noted earlier in these memoirs, Mr. Bryce, when occasion required it, for all his huge bulk, could move as agilely and noiselessly as that pre-eminently silent animal, the domestic cat. He had been so keyed up by the emotional stresses of the last few days that he threw himself into the adventure with all the zest of a schoolboy just being introduced into romance. The man was dodging through the trees a hundred yards or so ahead, and there was something so furtive about his movements that Bryce approached with more than his usual caution.

The man halted and glanced swiftly around. Bryce flattened himself against a handy tree, and fervently hoped that the shadow was thick enough to conceal him. The other patently had no idea that he was being followed, for, apparently quite satisfied with his hasty scrutiny, he dropped on his knees and commenced scraping the earth away with the point of a knife that had appeared in his hand with the magical suddenness of a conjuring trick. As the man worked away Bryce peeped out from his hiding-place and saw then that it was indeed Cumshaw. He watched fascinated. His heart was thumping away like the piston of a steam-engine, and some queer unnamed instinct told him that the chase was drawing to a close. Cumshaw was digging up something of vital importance; it might be the treasure itself or perhaps the key to it. But why should Cumshaw have gone so stealthily to work unless - ? "Unless he is going to cut me out of it," said Bryce to himself.

Abruptly the other straightened up and hugged something to his breast. It was covered with black loam, and at the distance Bryce could not tell what it was. He slipped stealthily from tree to tree until he had wormed his noiseless way right up to Cumshaw. Then, seeing that he had his man cut off should he attempt to escape, he stepped out into the open and laid a kindly hand on the fugitive's shoulder. Cumshaw turned in a flash, and, in the excitement of the moment, the earth-covered object slipped out of his hands and fell on the grass at his feet.

"Where have you been all this time?" Bryce asked jovially.

Cumshaw stared at him in a puzzled way. His face at first had shown all the symptoms of fear, but the moment Bryce spoke they faded out, to be replaced by a very obvious air of relief. Yet there was nothing of recognition in the man's eyes; they were full of a great blank wonder, like the eyes of a child who takes its first look at the teeming life beyond its doors. His forehead crinkled up as if he were trying to recall something that had slipped his memory.

"Who are you?" he said at length. "I ... I don't think I know you," and he brushed his forehead with a weak, ineffective gesture of the hand. It was then that Bryce noticed the matted, blood-stained condition of his hair and the big purple bruise that disfigured his temple. His quick mind guessed at what had happened, though, erroneously enough, he concluded that Cumshaw had received the blows in an encounter with the men who had been the original cause of the man's flight.

"You'd better come with me, Cumshaw," he said in the same soothing tone that he would have applied to a tired child.

"I'm going home," said Cumshaw with weak stubbornness. "I don't want to go with you."

"I'll take you home," said Bryce.

That he decided was the only thing he could do. Cumshaw was in no fit state to continue the search for his lost valley, and Bryce realised that it would not be safe to leave him uncared for. If he went home with Cumshaw he would be throwing his pursuers off the track. That would help him considerably. He had no fear that they would discover the valley during his absence; their attack on him showed that they had come to the end of their resources, and fancied that their only hope of touching any of the spoils was by forcing the secret out of Bryce. Of course it was quite on the cards that they would follow the car, but it was just as likely that they would make no definite move until they had solved the meaning of his change of plans.

Cumshaw was still standing like a man in a dream. Bryce placed his hand on the man's arm.

"Come along with me," he said. "I'll see that you get safely home."

He bent down quickly and picked up the loam-encrusted object that Cumshaw had dropped in the first moment of the encounter, Cumshaw followed his movements with troubled eyes, but did not interfere in any way. Bryce could see that the thing was a bit of wood, and on one piece of it, where the earth had been scraped off, there were letters scratched. He thrust it into his pocket, meaning to examine it more closely at his leisure.

Cumshaw walked to the car with him. He yielded to the stronger will without any show of resistance. All his own will-power seemed to have departed, and he obeyed Bryce with a child-like faith. Once in the car he slumped into the corner and closed his eyes. Bryce seized the opportunity thus given him to steal another look at the wood he had picked up. He scraped away what loam he could with his finger nail, and soon was able to make out two complete words.

"This'll have to wait," he said with a sigh, as he thrust it back into his pocket. "This bit of wood's got your name on it, Mr. Abel Cumshaw, and I'll bet all I ever owned that it's the key you've been hunting for."

He cranked up the car, and soon was speeding back to the high road. In his corner Mr. Cumshaw slept.

Ten minutes after they reached the main road another car swung out along the Ararat road. There were three men in it, the chauffeur and two passengers. One of the latter held his hand to a wounded shoulder, and swore at the chauffeur every time the car jolted and sent a quiver of pain through the wound.

In course of time Bryce's car came to a little hamlet on the Geelong to Colac road - a hamlet that must be nameless in this story. There he found the Albert Cumshaw of this tale, delivered his father into his care and told him all that had happened, suppressing only the episode of the finding of the wood. He found Albert Cumshaw easier to deal with than he had expected - as a matter of fact the younger man already knew much of his father's story - and the result of the conversation was that the search was held over, pending the elder Cumshaw's recovery.

Bryce remained the night with the Cumshaws, saw that a doctor was secured who would give skilled attention to the elder man, and then early in the morning set out for home. The day was very warm, and the cool breeze that presently sprang up from the ocean moved Bryce to motor down to the coast. At the worst it was only a few miles out of his road. At first he had no intention of making a stop at the heads, but the sea as he came within sight of it looked so cool and inviting that he was tempted to have a dip. He parked his car in the reserve, purchased a bathing suit at the local store and ambled down to the beach. It was only when he commenced to undress that he recollected that the wood was still in his pocket, so with rare caution he thrust it under the sand, quite satisfied that no one would dream of looking there. He had no idea that his pursuers were so close behind him; he was merely taking precautions against any casual tramp who might be tempted to run through his pockets.

Ten minutes later James Carstairs, explorer, gentleman and rolling stone, limped into the picture, and the story of The Lost Valley entered upon its penultimate phase.

PART III

THE FINDING OF THE LOST VALLEY

CHAPTER I

THE CYPHER

"You may smoke if you like, Mr. Cumshaw," Moira said graciously to our visitor.

I said nothing; instead I silently handed the man my cigar-case. He selected a weed with a discriminating care that I felt cast an unwarranted reflection on the quality of the cigars I smoked. I watched him in silence while he cut off the end with a neat, precise stroke of his penknife, lit the cigar and blew a cloud of blue smoke out of his mouth. All the time I was staring at him I could feel Moira's eyes on me, and I knew that she was wondering what made me so boorish and morose. Or, perhaps, with a woman's keen instinct for ferreting out the things she shouldn't know anything about, she guessed just what was the matter. To tell the truth I was just beginning to feel a little jealous. Frankly I considered that she was paying too much attention to Mr. Albert Cumshaw, and I hadn't two sharp eyes without seeing that he openly admired her. Of course I had turned down her overtures of reconciliation, and I think I told her plainly enough that there was no possibility of my falling in love with her again; but, if all that were perfectly true, I shouldn't have been jealous because the two of them took to making eyes at each other. The fact remained that I was a little hurt by what I saw, and I had to recognise, even though I ran counter to the promptings of my common-sense, that I wasn't as indifferent to her as I would have myself believe.

I brought myself back with a jerk to the matter in hand.

"What do you propose doing about the matter?" I asked of Cumshaw.

He did not reply immediately. His right little finger flipped the ash from off the end of his cigar, and then the dark curly head lifted and the glowing eyes looked straight into mine.

"What do I propose doing!" he repeated. "Well, if it was left to me," he said, after a contemplative pause, "I'd say the treasure's there, and the sooner we go after it the better. We know already that there's other people on the job - they killed Mr. Bryce and they made a mess of the Dad - and it's all right thinking, as Mr. Bryce did, that they've come to the end of their tether and are waiting for us to set the pace for them. There's been so many miracles in this play already that it doesn't do to risk the chance of any more. We've got no absolute guarantee that they won't stumble on the key to everything while we're wasting time here. You say you've got a cypher Mr. Bryce left you. Well, that cypher contains the position of the treasure; there's no doubt about that in my mind. Bradby carved it on the wood - neither he nor the Dad had any paper with them at the time - and from what I've heard of the man I'm confident that it's the kind of thing he would do. Then when Mr. Bryce got hold of it he burnt the wood and threw what was on it into a sort of cryptogram. One way and another he was pretty cautious when the fit took him, though I must say that when it was a question of his own life he wasn't so particular. It boils down to this. The Dad's out of the game for good and we've got to use our own wits. Within limits we've got a fair idea of the position of the valley, and, once we've solved the cypher, we'll probably have something more definite to go on."

"That," I remarked, "is supposing we do solve it. As far as I can see it's too weird for anything."

"Uncle," said Moira severely, "wouldn't have written it if he didn't think you could solve it. That's why he made it easy."

"If you think it's easy," I retorted, "take it yourself and see what you can make of it."

"That's a good idea," Cumshaw cut in, turning my own shaft against myself. "Suppose we all have a shot at it and see what we can make of it. We might get it all out and again we mightn't. When we get as far as we can we'll all pool our efforts, and maybe we'll make something out of it that way."

"An excellent suggestion, Mr. Cumshaw," Moira said, and darted a glance of triumph at me. It said as plainly as so many words that here was a champion for her, a man who would defend her against the whole world. Of course I ignored it. What man would do anything else under the circumstances? But there are some things, of which this was one, that the more one ignores them the more insistent as to their presence do they become. So, though I affected not to see Moira's little glance of triumph, it photographed itself upon my mind's eye and completely spoiled the evening for me.

"We'll get Jim here to type out a copy for you before you go, Mr. Cumshaw," she promised, "and you can see what you can make of it."

"Thanks," said the young man briefly. I had expected him to make a bigger mouthful of it than that, and I thought it odd that he did not. It struck me too as queer that he did not ask for a look at the cypher; an ordinary man would have known no peace until he had examined it in all its baffling details. As I was to learn, Mr. Cumshaw was no ordinary man, and, for a young chap of his age, had his emotions and inclinations under rather remarkable control.

I stood up. "If you want that cypher," I said, "I'll type it out now, and you can study it on the way home if you wish."

"It's very kind of you," Cumshaw murmured with a well-bred lack of enthusiasm.

"I think," said Moira, "that we'd all better adjourn to the study. I don't like to think of anyone being in there alone, especially at night. You see," she explained to Cumshaw, "the room hasn't been used since Uncle's death. He was killed in that very room ... in front of my eyes."

"I understand," said Cumshaw softly, and he rose to his feet and held the door open for Moira to pass out. She led the way to the study and unlocked the door. It had been a fad of hers ever since the tragedy to keep the room sealed, and, as I saw no reason for gainsaying her, I had never interfered. She switched on the light and we stood for a moment on the threshold, dazzled by the unaccustomed radiance. Nothing in the place had been touched - we had not disturbed anything during our search for Bryce's papers - and, save for the absence of some of the actors in the scene, it might have been the very night of the tragedy itself.

I broke the spell by walking into the room and proceeding to take the cover off the typewriter. The machine had not been used since its owner had died. Despite the manner in which I had lied to Bryce, I knew a thing or two about typewriters. As a matter of fact I transcribed the greater part of my father's three volumes of Solomon Island Ethnology on just such another machine. I sat down at the table and drew from my pocket the letter and the cypher, both of which I had thrust out of sight when Albert Cumshaw had been announced that afternoon.

"There's the cypher," I said, and I spread the sheet out on the table.

Cumshaw bent over it and read out aloud from beginning

to end.

"2@3; 5@3 &9; 3 5433-3/4 5@ 3 @75 L994 1/4;L 5@3 481/28;? 1/27; 1/443 8; & 8;3 - 31/41/2743 1/23:3; "335 31/41/25.5@3; "1/4/3 L843/5 ;945@3/4L41/42 1/4;95@34 &8;3 1/45 48?@5 1/4;?&31/2 59 5@3 043:8971/2 9;33/43)53;L8;? " 94 523&:3 "335.L8? 5@3;," he said, stumbling every now and then at the unfamiliar expressions.

"What do you make of it?" I asked.

He looked up at me with just the flicker of a smile about the corners of his mouth. "I can't say just yet," he replied. "All these things take time. You can't solve them in an instant."

"I thought we might," I said, with just the least hint of offensiveness in my tone. I don't know whether or not he noticed it, but if he did he was gentleman enough to ignore it.

"All right," I ran on, "I'll type this out if one of you'll read it to me. Go slowly, as I don't want to have any mistakes. It's bad enough to have to do it once without having to do it again."

"I'll read it," Cumshaw volunteered. I nodded to show my agreement. I then threaded the paper through and said, "I'm ready."

He began to read it very slowly and carefully, and I typed away as he spoke. I had just got the first four or five combinations down when Moira interrupted me.

"I knew you'd make a mess of it," she said coldly. "I told you so at the beginning." As a matter of fact she had said no such thing, but I let it pass.

"What's wrong?" I queried, looking up at her.

"I've been watching you," said she, "and you haven't depressed your figure lever once. You must have it all wrong. It'll just be simple letters instead of the signs."

I had been typing all the time with my eyes on the keyboard, and I hadn't once glanced at the finished work. Now I looked at it I saw that she was right. I had been typing letters all along when I should have been printing figures. And then something queer about the letters struck me. My heart gave a jump.

"Go on," I said huskily to Cumshaw. "Give me a few more."

He read out two or three more combinations and then I leaned back in the chair. "Look," I said triumphantly, "look what I've done!"

Two heads bobbed down over my work, stared at it for a moment, and then two pairs of eyes smiled at me.

"You've solved it by accident," said Cumshaw.

"I'm sorry for what I said," Moira said simply.

"It's just the simplest cypher in existence," I said. "You've got a keyboard with letters and figures on it. When you want letters you type straight out, and when you want figures you just depress the lever. Now look at this. That 5 is on the same key as T, @ is on H's key, 3 means E, and so on. When Bryce worked it out he simply pressed down the figure lever and left it down, and now to reverse the process all we've got to do is to hit the keys these signs are on and leave the lever alone. Simple, isn't it?"

"Very," said Cumshaw.

"Get it all out, Jim, quick!" said Moira with feminine impatience.

I did. I pressed 2 and I got W, and so on all along the keyboard, and when I had finished I pulled the sheet out and handed it to them. "Read it out, Moira," I said. "It's your turn."

"'When the Lone Tree, the hut door and the rising sun are in line measure seven feet east. Then face direct north, draw another line at right angles to previous one, extending for twelve feet. Dig then.'"

"If it hadn't been for you," said Cumshaw, "we wouldn't have found it. I congratulate you," and he held out his hand to me.

"Rubbish!" I said. "It was all a lucky accident." But all the same I took the proffered hand.

"We can go right on with it now," Moira cried joyously. "There's nothing to stop us."

"Only that we've got to find the valley yet," said Cumshaw gloomily. "My father made several attempts but couldn't locate it."

"You've got to bear in mind," I told them, "that we've got some information your father hadn't, strange though it seems."

"And that?" Cumshaw queried quickly.

"We're looking for a valley that's got a lone tree overlooking it. Your father didn't seem to be aware of that."

Cumshaw seized the paper and read it through quickly. "By the Lord Harry, you're right, Carstairs! That's one piece of information he didn't have. If he had known that when he went after the gold himself he'd have got it."

"Maybe he would," I said doubtfully.

"You don't seem too sure of it, Carstairs," Cumshaw remarked, with a sidelong glance at Moira.

"No more I am," I told him. "I don't like our chances either."

"But," he protested with a puzzled indrawing of his eyebrows, "as far as we're concerned it's as easy as falling off a log."

"Just as easy," I agreed, "providing our friends the enemy don't interfere. They don't seem to be the kind of men who rest on their oars, that is if we can judge anything from their past exploits."

"You're right there, Carstairs," Cumshaw said. "I never gave them a thought, but I see now that they're likely to prove a pretty active menace to our safety."

"That," I said, turning to Moira, "cuts out all possibility of your coming with us. You can't be running into danger."

"Can't I just," she said with an assertive toss of her head, "and, whether I can or not, I'm going," she finished.

I looked at Cumshaw. I could not tell from his expression whether he was pleased or sorry. His face was as devoid of emotion as that of a china doll.

"What do you think about it?" I asked him straight out.

He glanced at me in his turn with a curious baffling light in his dark eyes, and I felt as if he had stripped my soul bare of all pretences and was reading my thoughts in all their nakedness.

"I should think," he said at length with an air of absolute impartiality, "that Miss Drummond is the mistress of her own actions and neither you nor I have any right to dictate what she is to do."

"Have it your own way then," I said, with difficulty suppressing my rising anger. "But if anything goes wrong remember that I warned you beforehand."

"I'll remember that," Moira said, and she favored Cumshaw with a little smile of gratitude. She never smiled at me like that, not even in those far-away days when we were all the world to each other or thought we were. Which in the end amounts to much the same thing.

"Well, if you don't mind," said Cumshaw, breaking an awkward silence, "I'll go home now and think matters over. And then to-morrow we'll decide what to do."

"Home?" I echoed. "I thought - " And then I stopped.

"I'm staying in town," he said with a smile. "That's what I meant when I said home."

"In that case," I said, "you'll be handy whenever we want you. You'd better leave your address in case we want you in a hurry."

He scribbled his address - a leading city hotel - on a blank card and handed it to me. I glanced at it and then thrust it into my pocket. When I looked up again he was holding Moira's hand in his, just a trifle longer than convention demanded I thought, and saying something to her that I did not catch. She smiled in return, a dazzling smile, and said quite distinctly, "Please call whenever you feel inclined. There is no need for us to stand on ceremony with each other now we're partners."

I saw him to the door. At the threshold he turned and spoke with one foot on the step and the other on the ground, taking up that attitude of unaffected ease that gives an air of friendliness to even the most formal conversation.

"I'm rather pleased I met you, Carstairs," he said. "In one way and another I've heard a lot about you, and I think you've got the kind of level head we'll need before we've seen this business through."

"Thank you," I replied. I was nearly going to say 'Soft words butter no parsnips,' but my common-sense came to my aid just in time to prevent me making a fool of myself. He held out his hand, and I took it in the spirit in which he had offered it to me. Nevertheless I was absurdly jealous of the man, though Heaven knows I hadn't the least reason to be. I could see with half an eye that he had made a good impression on Moira, and the way she had spoken to him, especially that last remark of hers, showed me that she was egging him on. It didn't matter one single solitary damn to me. I had told her clearly and definitely that we were business partners and that love was altogether out of the question. Yet here was I, the moment a potential rival appeared on the scene, behaving for all the world like a spoilt child. And, like a spoilt child, for my own good I needed someone to bring me sharply and suddenly to my bearings.

Cumshaw bade me a cheerful good-night. I saw his lithe figure swing along through the sub-tropical darkness of a moonless summer night. Then the latch on the gate clicked with the ringing sound of metal striking against metal. I closed the door and went inside.

Moira was standing in the study just as I had left her, standing as motionless and devoid of life as a statue of carven stone. I don't think she heard me at first.

"Well," I said conversationally, "how is it now?"

She turned at the sound of my voice and faced me squarely. I could see that her eyes were bright with unshed tears, and something inside of me moved me with a sudden impulse to go up to her. I placed my hands on her shoulders and was amazed to find how unsteady they were. They trembled, my hands trembled! And yet they used to tell me in the old Island days that I hadn't a nerve in my body.

I was quite prepared for anything except what really happened. I could feel a sort of tension in the atmosphere, and I expected her to do something theatrical. But she didn't. She backed away from me, but she didn't go far. The table was behind her.

I don't know how long we stood looking at each other. It seemed a lifetime to me, and the silence was the sort that a man feels it sacrilege to break.

"You make it very hard for me, Jim," Moira said calmly. The tears were still in her eyes, but her voice was under excellent control. It didn't vibrate a note. She looked at me as she spoke, looked me straight in the eyes, and I think it was then that I began to realise what an ass I had been making of myself.

"How do I make it hard?" I asked. My voice was curiously low, almost husky in fact. I rather think she noticed it and took heart therefrom. A man is very easy to handle when he is not quite sure of himself.

"I've got to pretend," she said in answer to my question. "Pretend that you are nothing to me when - "

She stopped short. It seemed almost as if she regretted that she had said so much.

"Go on," I urged.

"There's not much to say," she continued. "I just want to tell you, to tell you in such a way that you'll believe me, that if I've treated you shamefully I've suffered for it. I can't make any reparation for it; you were quite right in saying that it is too late now to alter things. I just want you to know that I'm sorry. I can't say much more than that, though I don't want to take any credit for it now, seeing that it's been practically forced out of me."

I remembered the way she had been standing when I came in, the tears in her eyes, and the way she had backed out of my reach the moment I put my hands on her shoulders. It would have been so easy for her to have done the other thing, but she hadn't, and I admired her all the more for it. She might easily have captured me in the first flush of emotion, but she had instead given me time to think and a chance to get away if I wanted to. There was something in her attitude that appealed to my sense of fair play and at the same time prevented me from in any way misinterpreting her last remark.

"Moira," I said, "were you crying when I came in just now?"

Her lip trembled a little as she asked, "Why do you want to know?"

"Because," I said slowly, "I've solved one riddle already to-night, and I've a mind to solve another before I go to bed."

"I was crying," she admitted, "only I didn't mean you to see."

"And why was that?"

"I thought you might imagine I was just doing it."

I knew what she meant; there was no need for her to explain further. She didn't want to influence me in any way; whatever I did must be done of my own free will.

"I'm beginning to understand," I said slowly.

"Then you'll forgive?" she said quickly, and one hand went up to her throat as if she were choking.

I nodded and impulsively she held out her hand to me. I did not take it, and she half-turned so that I would not see what was in her eyes.

"Can't we even be friends?" she said, with a queer little catch in her words.

Something snapped in my head at that, and the words I had been holding back all the evening came to my lips in a rush of speech.

"I didn't mean you to take it that way," I said desperately. "I wouldn't shake hands because ... that's not what I want. It's too stand-offish. I'm going to do more than forgive, and we're going to me more than friends, if you still want me."

"You know I want you," she said softly with her head bowed shyly and the blushes rising in her cheeks.

I took her in my arms and kissed her.

CHAPTER II

OVER THE HILLS AND FAR AWAY

Once we had definitely fixed the date of our departure we lost no time in making ready. As the days went by I began to see more and more clearly that it was just as well I had thrown in my lot with Moira and young Cumshaw. Neither of them had the least idea of organisation, and they seemed to think that things just happened of their own accord. Moira couldn't see anything else but the glamor and romance of the adventure, and I found that, for all his cleverness, Albert Cumshaw did not know what was essential to the expedition and what wasn't.

"We can't start off like a picnic party," I said to them on one occasion, "and just wander on until we come to a likely spot. We've got to have everything planned out right down to the last box of matches and the last cartridge."

Cumshaw drew a deep breath. "Cartridges!" he said, "Are you talking figuratively?"

"No," I answered. "I'm speaking literally. It might yet be the case of the last cartridge. You must remember that, even if we get the gold and come back here in safety, we're still not out of the wood. We're not safe until our friends the enemy are removed from our paths for ever."

"You mean that they must be killed?" Moira demanded.

"I don't mean anything of the kind," I answered. "As a matter of fact I've got a perfect horror of killing people. It makes such a mess, and I'm naturally a rather tidy person."

Cumshaw laughed softly, but Moira bit her lip, though she made no reply to what I had said.

"Now, while we're talking about it," I ran on, "I just want to impress on you the fact that we aren't going off into the bush - not the kind of bush that you read about in books, where it's all scrub and myall blacks and things like that. Most of the time we'll be within coo-ee of civilisation. Most of Western Victoria's pretty well settled, and it's just the luck of the game and the formation of the country that this valley's remained so long hidden away. We'll be near enough to people all the time to be noticeable if we do anything remarkable. We've got to go to work so that we'll attract as little attention as possible. We'll want food, enough for several weeks, I suppose, and we've got to get it and take it with us, and do it all in such a way that nobody's going to wonder what we're after. Another thing that that reminds me of. Miss Drummond here had better keep out of sight as long as she can. We two can manage to escape observation, but people always want to know what a woman's doing in it when there's anything suspicious happening."

"If you mean by that that you think I can be turned back at the last moment, you're making a mistake," Moira informed me.

"I don't mean that," I said calmly, "but I want to take every precaution that I can. I'm in charge of this expedition, elected by three votes to nothing, and I'm going to run things the way I think best. It mightn't be the best way in the end, but that's quite another matter. I haven't wandered across the world from Yokohama to the White Nile and from the Klondyke to the Solomons without knowing how to organise an expedition."

"You're right there," Cumshaw acknowledged. "You're the

only one amongst us who's had practical experience. In future what you say goes."

"That's the spirit," I said briskly. "What have you to say, Moira?"

"You know best," she answered. "As long as you don't leave me out altogether I'll agree to anything, but I want to take my share of the risk too."

"Apparently," I remarked, "everyone's afraid that everybody else'll have the lion's share of the fighting. Well, if I can fix it, there'll not be any fighting at all."

"What do you mean?" Cumshaw asked interestedly.

"That's nothing to do with the situation at present," I informed him. "You'll all see when the time's ripe. Now what's next?"

"There's nothing more that I know of," Cumshaw volunteered.

"And you, Moira?"

"I think I've got everything fixed," she answered.

"That means we can start at the end of the week," I said with satisfaction. "It looks as if fortune's turning our way at last."

The three of us laughed together, and Cumshaw I think it was who said, "Success to the expedition!" It sounded very nice, and we were all so sure that things were going to turn out well. But there was one little point that all of us had overlooked, and that was destined in one way and another to upset our plans to a remarkable extent.

Profiting by Bryce's experience, I decided to leave the car at home, as I realised that we would have to abandon it sooner or later, and nothing is so apt to set foolish people talking as an apparently ownerless car. I resolved on making our head-quarters at the spot where by all accounts the unlamented Mr. Bradby had met his death. For one thing all the later developments of the chase had centred round that one spot, and Bryce himself had gone there unhesitatingly by the shortest and most direct route he knew of. I couldn't see at the time where I could find a better jumping-off place. To say the least it was a fixed point from which to start exploring, and we had the comforting knowledge, though it might not be of any practical use to us, that the valley itself was within two or three days' march. With it as the centre we would have to cast a circle with a radius of anything up to fifty miles, and then somewhere within the enclosed area we might, or might not, find the elusive vale that held the treasure.

We approached the rendezvous by widely divergent routes. It was a rather extravagant precaution, no doubt, but then I wasn't taking any risks that I could possibly avoid. The murderous gentlemen who were quite certainly on our track were a power to be reckoned with, and at the same time we had to keep our eyes open for the law itself. It was all right for Bryce to say that he was playing within the law - quite possibly he was - but I had no idea of paying any percentage to the Crown. I was rather hazy on the matter myself, though I seemed to have heard somewhere or other that the Government always gobbled a big share of the loot in the case of treasure trove. At any rate the quieter we kept the expedition the less likelihood there was of us having to pay anything at all.

Moira was to travel with me from Murtoa, and Cumshaw decided to train as far as Landsborough - the recently opened Crowlands to Navarre railway would take him that far - and then do the rest across the hills on foot. His was the longer and more difficult route, and I had intended at first to take it myself, for reasons that have nothing at all to do with this tale; but he was so insistent, and at one stage threatened so much unpleasantness, that I gave into him, if only for the sake of peace. Before we started I had another talk with Moira and endeavored to dissuade her from accompanying us, but she very calmly told me that she had additional reasons now for going with us. There was sure to be trouble, she admitted that much; but then wasn't her place by my side, more especially if things weren't all they should be? Her logic left much to be desired, but it had the one merit of achieving its object. It was devastating; it completely crushed all my arguments and left me without a leg to stand on.

The late March of the year 1919 saw the three of us at the rendezvous, which we had reached without incident of any sort. Contrary to our expectations the other party had not been sighted, and the outlook was certainly auspicious. For all that I felt worried. Everything was going along too swimmingly, and I had a queer feeling that we would meet with trouble very shortly, if only to even things up. Ease and success can only be won after much expenditure of blood and tears; there is not a thing in life worth trying for that can be bought with a minimum of effort. The greater the prize, the greater the price one must pay; always one pays, with health, with limbs, sometimes with life itself.

During the time Moira and I had been travelling together I had slept of a night with one eye more or less open, and the strain of being constantly on the alert was just beginning to tell on me. As a consequence I was very pleased when Cumshaw suggested that we should take watch and watch about. I agreed, with the reservation that I must always be on guard for the dawn-watch. I didn't explain why I was so anxious to take that particular watch, and, though I noticed Moira looking curiously at me, she made no remark. I knew from experience that men are at their sleepiest about four o'clock in the morning, and an attack can be successfully launched then that would fail at any other hour of the day or night. I had yet to test Cumshaw on active service, so I claimed the four o'clock stretch for my own. It doesn't hurt to be careful; I've never yet met anyone who was sorry he had taken precautions.

We camped within a hundred yards of the creek, and after supper Cumshaw and I sprawled on the grass and talked. Moira had retired to an improvised tent we had fashioned for her, and, as it was just out of earshot, we were free to speak our thoughts. I had not seen Cumshaw for the better part of two weeks - he had started from his own place and come right on from there without calling on me again - and I hoped that he might have some further news for me. I asked him casually how his father was getting on.

"Right enough," he said, blowing a cloud of smoke out of his mouth. "Some days you wouldn't think there was a thing wrong with him. He'll talk pretty lucidly at times, but it isn't anything that can be of any use to us. He doesn't seem to have taken much notice of the position of the valley, he apparently thought at the time that it would be very simple to pick it up again, and I fancy that Bradby must have confirmed him in that view. He couldn't have taken into account the way they had twisted about in the mountains. It's the simplest thing in the world to lose yourself here, the more so if you're confident you know your way."

"You've about struck it there," I said. "I just want to give you a little piece of advice, and I hope you won't take it amiss. I don't want to talk about this expedition any more than I can help for two reasons. One's this: I don't wish to cause Miss Drummond any more uneasiness than is absolutely necessary. You know as well as I do that there's a big chance of the lot of us being wiped out just about the time we get within sight of the end. I wouldn't be surprised if they let us walk into a trap and finished us at their leisure. As for the other reason - well, it's never safe to say that you're alone anywhere. If we raise our voices above whispers here we might be giving away valuable information. So just let us keep watch on our tongues. More hopes have been ruined and more chances of success spoilt by gabbling tongues than by any other dozen causes all rolled together."

"I can quite understand that," Cumshaw said, between puffs at his pipe. It was one of those neat little affairs with a round bowl, a spick-and-span pipe that had burnt an even color and that shone as brightly as the day he bought it. My pipe was a sorrier article; it was battered and blackened, and one side of the bowl was down beneath the level of the other, showing that it had been lighted oftener with a blazing brand than with the orthodox matches. In a way it was like its owner; it had been tested by fire and had survived the test. If I were philosophical - but then I wasn't, and that's about all there is to it.

"I didn't go to Landsborough," Cumshaw said after a pause. "I missed my train at Ararat, and so I came on to Great Western. It's much the shorter way. I wish you had known of it before."

"I'm all the better pleased you came that way," I told him. "It will help to disorganise the chase."

He bent over, picked up a live coal in his bare fingers and applied it to his pipe before replying.

"I rather think," he said slowly, "that it will have just the opposite effect."

"You can't have any nerves in those fingertips of yours," I said. "Why will it?"

"I don't seem to have any, do I? I think I saw one of the men at Great Western."

"You don't know them," I said. "How could you?"

"Mr. Bryce described them in his letter," Cumshaw answered. "This man fitted the description of one of them, a dark sort of chap."

"Spanish type?" I queried.

Cumshaw nodded. "I wonder why it is," he ran on, "that we're always more suspicious of that sort of man than, say, a fair type?"

"Relic of the Armada, I suppose," I suggested. "Tell me all about the man you saw."

"I was coming along the roadside," Cumshaw began, "past one of the vineyards, when I noticed a man working close at hand. I was just going to pass by when it struck me that he was the only person about. I thought that rather queer and I gave him a second look. Then I saw that he wasn't digging, as I had thought at first, but that he was scratching aimlessly at the ground. One of those queer feelings that seem altogether unrelated to fact crept over me. Call it second sight or any other fancy name you please, the fact remains that I suddenly knew - not thought, mind you; I knew - that he did not want me to notice him and that he was pretending to be one of the workmen, just so that I would pass him by without more than a cursory glance. When I came to think it over afterwards, I remembered that it struck me when first I saw him that he was the only man I had seen in the vineyards for miles. Of course I had that idea in my mind when I looked at him the second time. That doesn't explain how I understood that I was the very man he did not want to see. He had his head bent down naturally, his hat well drawn over his face, and he went on scratching and scraping as if his very life depended on the energy with which he worked. I didn't get more than a passing glimpse of him, and that wasn't too good - you can't go over to a man and pull off his hat just because he looks suspicious - but I'd swear on a stack of Bibles that he's one of the men we'll have to deal with."

"Perhaps so," I said. "At any rate I'm not going to allow chance workers in the fields to rob me of my night's rest."

"No more am I," assented Cumshaw. "So you don't think there's any likelihood - ."

"I don't think anything at all," I cut in. "I take proper

precautions, that's all."

He made no comment on my unceremonious interruption, but the strange half-smile he gave me showed that he realised in part at least how his story had affected me. As a matter of fact I was more perturbed than I cared to admit. I had been thinking things over all day, and it had just occurred to me that, seeing we had heard nothing of them since Bryce's death, it was quite possible that they were even now following up the false clue that he had laid for them, and which one of them had got away with the night of the burglary. If that were so, why had they come back and killed Bryce? It was a curious enough situation, and the more I thought about it the more I became convinced that I was right. Our immunity so far was due solely to the fact that the others were well occupied with the faked plan they had stolen on that memorable evening. Now on top of that Albert Cumshaw must come with this circumstantial story of his and upset all my deductions. The strange part of it was, though my reason told me that he had been a victim of his own brilliant imagination, part of my mind - that part that believed in second sight and banshees and were-wolves, and stuff of that sort - told me that he was not so very much wrong after all.

"I'll get to sleep," he said, interrupting the train of my thoughts. "I'll be fresh when my turn comes for guard."

"Tell me," I said, for the matter had been puzzling me all night, "where did you learn to light your pipe with red-hot coals?"

"Oh, that," he said with a laugh. "I saw you doing it earlier in the evening, and I made up my mind that what you did I could do."

"Then it must have burnt you."

"Horribly," he said with a grimace. "Good-night."

CHAPTER III

THE PROMISED LAND

"This," I remarked, "is the sort of country Adam Lindsay Gordon would have loved. No man but he could do justice to it."

"We've been out seven days," said Cumshaw, "we've travelled God knows how many miles, we've climbed up a Hades of a lot of mountains, and I don't think there's a blind creek for twenty miles that we haven't followed to the end and back again, and at the end of it all we're no nearer the Valley than we were when we started. Gordon might have made an epic out of it, but I'm hanged if I'm poet enough to appreciate the country or philosopher enough to ignore the sheer physical discomforts of the journey."

"If you'd been through the things I've been through," I asserted, "if you'd been in New Guinea when there was a gold-strike on and had to climb hundreds of feet up a straight cliff to get to the fields, hanging on all the time to creepers as thick as your wrist, you'd think this was just Paradise. If you'd been with me in the sweltering Solomon Island jungle, where every breath you took made the perspiration stand out on your forehead in big beads, or up in the Klondyke when it was fifty below and a man's own breath turned into ice about his mouth, you'd know what life really meant. Here you're in the Garden of Victoria; you see sights that knock some of the beauty spots of the world into a cocked hat, and all you can do is growl at the country. You can't expect to go up and down the mountain side in a lift or anything of the sort."

"It's all very well for you to talk like that," he objected. "You're used to this kind of life; we're not. That makes all the difference."

"So it seems," I said. "But I haven't the slightest intention of giving in yet. As a matter of fact I rather think we've been a little too sure that we were on the right track. We haven't been as careful as we might. We've gone along blindly."

"What do you mean?" he demanded.

"Just this. We've been so infernally confident that we only had to find a clump of wattle and a lone tree, and we were there. Now that lone tree must be somewhere on the east side of the valley, and, despite the fact that it's on high ground, it's so hidden that we wouldn't see it until we were almost on top of it. It might be perfectly visible from inside the valley, and at the same time be hidden from the outside by another hill. As for the wattle, has it ever struck you that wattle only begins to spring into bloom about the end of August? It's almost April now, and you wouldn't find anything but just a mass of green bushes."

"If there was a valley, which same I'm beginning to doubt," Cumshaw said doggedly, "we'd have found it before this."

"I don't know what Miss Drummond is cooking for our tea," I remarked irrelevantly, "but it smells good."

"If you think you can put me off that way," Cumshaw said, "you're mighty mistaken. I'm tired of it all, and for two pins -"

"You know very well," I cut in, "that I haven't one pin, let alone two."

"You apparently don't understand that I'm perfectly serious."

"Yes, I do. I'm serious too. I'm quite satisfied that we haven't been going about things in the right way. We've made mistakes, and it's up to us to find out what those mistakes are and go over the ground again."

"I'll give it another week," said Cumshaw, "and if we haven't found anything by then we might as well retire, for you can bet your sweet life we never will."

I didn't answer him immediately. I was sprawling on the grass, on my back, with my eyes turned to the west, and something in the color of the sky surrounding the setting sun caught and held my attention. Curiously enough it made me think of Gordon and "The Sick Stockrider" - it must have been floating through my mind when I began to talk - and it needed very little effort of imagination to see -

> The deep blue skies wax dusky and the tall green trees grow dim, And the sickly, smoky shadows through the sleepy sunlight swim, And on the very sun's face weave their pall,

but there were no blue skies or green trees. The heavens were just a dull slate-grey with streaks of smoke-colored cloud scurrying across from the west, and the trees that might have been green in a better light were black and gaunt, like weird spectres which had taken on wild shapes and unorthodox hues. There was just the slightest suggestion of chill in the atmosphere, and that, combined with the scurrying clouds, made me study the sky with growing anxiety.

"If that's not a storm brewing," I said, pointing skywards, "I'm anything you like to call me."

Cumshaw cocked one eye in the direction indicated. "It does look like it," he said lazily, after a prolonged study of the sky.

I looked him up and down as best I could. One can't survey a man too well when lying on one's back; but something in the glance and more that I gave him, struck him as being so odd that he sat up and stared at me. I made no movement.

"Well?" he queried at length.

"It's just the other way round," I said in my most aggravating tone.

He looked at the sky again at that, and then turned his dark eyes on me. "I can see it's going to be a fine old storm," he said, "but I don't understand why you're worrying about it."

"I'm not," I said a trifle untruthfully. I was worrying, but not as much as he seemed to think. Ordinarily I would have told him just what I fancied was wrong, but this time I didn't fancy anything. For all I could say to the contrary there was just an ordinary April storm brewing over across the hills, and presently the thunder would begin, and then the lightning, and after that the rain; still I felt like a man who is on the verge of a great discovery, on the brink of finding that something that means all the difference in the world between success and failure. Even now when I come to consider calmly the emotions of that hour I cannot say that what I have just written down is a true description of my feelings and thoughts. What happened later that same night has had its effect on my memory and has mixed itself inextricably with my earlier recollections. All this about my fancying that the storm meant more than a storm usually means may be due to the fact that, but for it, the momentous event itself would never have occurred.

I do know that I was a little doubtful about the security of the improvised tent that sheltered Moira, and I think I must have showed a little of that anxiety in my face. That perhaps was what struck Cumshaw and led him to make the remark that he did.

Presently Moira called us to tea, and we hauled ourselves up from the grass and went over to her. The fire was burning up brightly and threw the tent and the surrounding trees into bold relief. It made the sky look even darker and more threatening than before. The scurrying clouds had all passed away by now, but in their train came thicker and heavier ones, big black things that rolled slowly across the evening sky with the heavy implacability of Fate. They moved like the advancing vanguard of a wild army of infamy, and soon had shut out altogether the dying light of day and the growing radiance of the silver stars. The sudden chill of thirty minutes previously had passed like a swift breath of wind into the limbo of lost and forgotten things, and in its place had grown a deadly hot oppressiveness that somehow reminded me of the sweltering dampness of those Gaudalcanar forests I had so recently described to Cumshaw. It filled us with something of its own torpor, so much so that we ate languidly, and when we spoke at all we spoke in monosyllables.

The storm broke almost without warning. There was just one low premonitory growl of thunder, the sky was split by a yellow sword of lightning, and then the rain came pouring down in the way that can be best described as the bursting of the flood-gates of heaven. At that our torpor vanished and we made an unceremonious rush for the poor shelter afforded by the tent, bringing with us what was left of our meal. The tent had not been constructed with a view to holding more than one; at its poor best it was but a rough shelter from the night dew. We had never intended it to keep out the rain; it had not entered our heads as even a remote possibility. I, perhaps, as the only one of the three who had had any practical experience of out-door life, should have kept just such a chance in mind. The fact remains that I overlooked it, and I can't say that then or at any other time was I sorry for my miscalculation.

I had lived so long in the tropics that the rain that came seemed to me the veriest drizzle, but the others had their own opinion, as I learnt the moment I said what I thought. Cumshaw remarked that it was the devil of a downpour, and Moira expressed her idea in less forcible though more polite terms. It was no use my saying that if I were in Port Moresby or Samarai the rain would have gone through the thin fabric of the tent like a rifle bullet through butter-cloth. They pointed out with equal truth that the present rain was dribbling through even as it was, and that a quarter of an hour more would see us saturated.

Whether we would or not must remain a mystery. No doubt we would have found out sooner or later had it not come on to blow. The thunder had ceased and the lightning flashed less frequently, now that the rain had set in, but the wind began to rise, and almost on the last clap of thunder I felt the wall of the tent shiver under the impact of the blast. It occurred to me in one of those flashes of memory that we sometimes have in moments of tension that we had not troubled about running up guy-ropes, and there was nothing now to hold the tent if the wind caught it squarely. Scarcely had the thought formed in my mind than an extra fierce blast caught the light fabric, shook it as a Newfoundland dog would shake a small terrier it had picked up in its mouth, and then, before we knew what had happened, the wind had whirled the tent away like a child's balloon, leaving us standing bareheaded, shivering and exposed to all the force of the elements. I left Moira with Cumshaw and groped about in the darkness, hoping to find our missing tent, but I might as well have been hunting for the proverbial needle in a bundle of hay for all the chance I had. I merely got wet through, so much so that I changed by mind completely about the force of Victorian storms, and when at last I found my way back to the others I was sopping from the sole of my boots to the top of the woe-begone hat I had hurriedly thrust on my head. As matters stood I could not get any wetter, and I supposed that Cumshaw was in much the same state. Nevertheless there was Moira to think of, and the sooner we got to shelter of some sort, a cave on the hillside or even a tolerably thick bush, the better it was going to be for all of us. I shouted this to Cumshaw - it was very hard to hear now that the gale had risen and was blowing everything to ribbons - and he understood me only after a couple of attempts. So I took Moira by one chill wet hand and Cumshaw took the other, and thus in the darkness and the steady soaking rain began our hunt for shelter of some sort.

I haven't an idea how far we walked. We just kept on and on, and really I think we did not notice the storm so much as if we had been standing still. Most of the time our attention was too taken up with feeling our way, for the ground was very slippery and more than once I almost lost my footing, to give more than a passing thought to personal discomfort. It was too dark to see more than an inch or so in front of us, and even then we saw nothing more than a black wall that constantly receded as we advanced and yet was still as near as ever in the end. I don't think any of us realised that we had drifted into a gully or a track of some sort until I put out a tentative hand and felt a wall of bushes dead in front of me. I pulled back with a jerk, but my sudden movement startled the others, and in the flurry of the moment they did the very thing I had been trying to avoid. They slipped and I went with them. I had sense enough to release Moira's hand the moment I felt the drag of her body, and then, before I quite knew what had happened. I found I was whirling along in the mud, cavorting down the side of something that looked, or felt - for I couldn't see, as I've already stated - very much like the edge of a precipice. I brought up, just when I was beginning to wonder how much further I had to fall, by colliding with something that felt very like a hedge of brambles. There I lay in the soaking rain, with the mud plastered thickly on my face, and every bit of breath knocked out of my body.

Somehow it seemed quieter down here. The wind still whistled and roared, but it was some feet or more above my head and it touched me not. Presently I began to sit up and wonder where I was and what had happened and what had become of the others. I felt very stiff and wet and dirty, and my right knee ached more than I liked. I was just on the point of staggering to my feet and feeling my way to leveller ground, when quite close to me I heard something very like a moan. I dropped on my knees at that and put out a tremulous hand. My fingers touched something soft and cold, and then I realised that it was a human face - Moira's, judging by the tangle of hair. I put my hand under the head and raised it up. A heavy mass of loose hair fell damply about my arm, and I knew then that it was my sweetheart I held. She stirred a little and moaned again. I was in a quandary. Clearly something must be done, but how or what I could no more say that I could fly. The night and the storm had swallowed Cumshaw up for the time being, but, beyond wondering vaguely what had become of him, I never gave him a thought. All my life long I'd been too used to men taking care of themselves to worry myself much about my missing colleague. But Moira's case was insistent and called for immediate attention. If there had been any shelter handy, even the rudest of bark humpies, I would have known what to do, and, what is more, I would have done it on the instant. Obviously the only course I could take was to crawl in under the ledge or precipice, or whatever it was, down which we had fallen and trust to the overhang - if there was any - and the few bushes that I had crashed through as I spun down, to keep the worst of the rain off us.

Accordingly I rose to my feet and lifted Moira up in my arms. She was a greater weight than I had thought, and that and my own condition caused me to walk with the uneven steps of a drunken man. At last I found some sort of recess in the side of the slope - I came across it more by accident than of set purpose - and there I crouched with Moira between me and the wall. The rain whirled in on me, and, if possible, I got a trifle wetter than before, but I had the satisfaction of knowing that my body kept both the rain and the wind away from her. It was a tedious enough job, holding the unconscious girl in my arms, and more than once I felt like dropping her, only that I recollected in time that I was crouching ankle deep in mud. I am stronger than the average, and I have had my body trained in hard schools, but even that has not made a Hercules of me. I was more than glad when she opened her eyes, or, rather, when she moved a little in my arms and then spoke.

She was not hurt much, she said in answer to my question, but she felt stiff in every limb, and the dampness seemed to have soaked through to her very bones. How was I, and what had happened?

I answered the two questions in almost the same breath. Brevity is not only the soul of wit, but it is the sole method of carrying on a conversation when both parties are wet and shivering.

"Have you any idea where we are?" Moira asked.

I shook my head and then, remembering that my answer was unintelligible in the darkness, I said, "I haven't. We fell over a cliff or a precipice, and that's all I can say about it."

"Why," she said, "you're shivering!" And she put out her hand to touch me. Her fingers came to rest on my arm, and I could feel her stiffen in the dark.

"Jim, why did you do it?" she demanded, with yet a curious softness in her voice.

"Do what?" I fenced.

"As if I don't know that you're in your shirt sleeves. That's your coat that's wrapped round me."

"What if it is?"

"You shouldn't have done it. You'll catch your death of cold."

"Much chance there is of that," I grunted.

She was silent for a time, and then I felt her arms about me, and I realised that she was trying to place my coat about my shoulders.

"If that's what you're after," I said, "I'll put it on. But you'll catch cold yourself."

She made no direct answer, but I heard something that sounded curiously like a sob.

Presently she moved up closer to me and a soft voice whispered in my ear, "Jim, I'll be warmer if you'll let me snuggle up to you. It's a long time since last ... I didn't deserve it then."

I reached out in the darkness and drew her towards me. With her tired head resting on my shoulder we waited for the dawn.

It was a long time coming, how long I cannot say, for in my then state of nervous tension the hours dragged with the awful unendingness of eternity. At last the black wall of night cracked into streaks of grey, looking for all the world like feeble sun-rays filtering through the chinks in the roof of a deserted house. Moira stirred a little, and I saw in one hasty glance that her wet hair was streaming about her face and her saturated dress was caked with black mud.

I held her off at arm's length and looked her over quizzically. Then we each laughed outright at the sight the other presented.

"You're wet through, Moira," I said, "and you look as if you've been having a mud-bath. All the same you're a brick to have stood it all the way you have."

"I'm not and I haven't," she said cryptically, and silenced my further objections with a kiss.

When I looked out on the world again it was to see that the day had already broken, and a dirty and bedraggled Albert Cumshaw was making his way towards us with slow and painful steps.

CHAPTER IV

WE ENTER THE VALLEY

I cannot explain why just at that instant my heart gave a thump. There was nothing for it to thump about. Cumshaw, toiling up the slope, for all his woe-begone look, was the most ordinary figure imaginable, and there was nothing in the landscape to excite or rivet attention. It was a white dawn, and, though the rain had ceased long before, everything was still dull and grey. In the hollows the mist lingered and hung between us and the further view like a great white curtain. That and the advancing Albert Cumshaw completed the picture, a picture that was neither interesting nor sensational. Yet at the sight, as I've already stated, my heart jumped queerly and unaccountably. Do coming events really ever cast their shadows before them? Are we sometimes granted visions of "the things beyond the dome?" I do not know, and, even if I did, I would not care to express a definite opinion in my own case. I have seen things dangerously like coincidences happen so often in my own experience that I have grown chary of either affirming or denying that there is something more than chance at the bottom of it all. Still the fact remains that twice within twenty-four hours the same queer feeling crept over me, and on each occasion the course of events proved that it was premonition. But that is running a shade ahead of the story.

I ran down the slope to meet Cumshaw, and the first thing I noticed was that there was a great livid bruise across his right temple.

"You've got a nasty knock there on your forehead," I greeted him, in the casual self-contained fashion of the men who live in the open.

He answered me with one of those laughs that are nothing more than almost soundless chuckles.

"Is it hurting?" I enquired with a trace of anxiety in my voice.

"Hurting, hell!" he said impolitely. "Of course it is."

"How did you do it? Was it an accident?"

"I don't look as if I did it just for amusement, do I?" he snarled.

"It hasn't improved your temper, my lad," I said under my breath. Aloud I remarked: "We're all in much the same boat. Miss Drummond's had a stiff time of it, and I've got all my bruises where you can't see them, but I can assure you that they hurt all the same."

At the mention of Moira a shadow passed over his face. Frankly I could not quite understand his attitude towards her. At first I was rather of the opinion that he was in love with her, but latterly I hadn't been so sure, for he had had the decency to suppress his feelings once he found how the land lay. The mere mention of her name calmed him down wonderfully. He even seemed a little ashamed of his outbursts of temper.

"I might have remembered that I wasn't the only one in the party," he said. "But then I came a fearful cropper, and on top of it I've been out in the rain all night."

"We were a little luckier." I told him. "We found an overhang and that kept off most of the rain. All the same I wouldn't mind a chance of drying myself."

"And we're likely to get that," he said with some asperity. "All our goods are God knows how many miles behind. I've got a box of matches in my pocket, but they're just about as useful here as they would be at the bottom of the sea."

"Come now," I said, "it's not as bad as all that. We've got a lady to take care of, and we've got to shuffle our brains about a bit and see what we can do. We'll never get anywhere by standing still railing at our fate."

"Well, you're in charge, Carstairs," he told me. "It's up to you."

"It is," I admitted, "and as the first step towards success I might point out to you that the mist is lifting."

He wheeled round at that with greater agility than I expected, seeing that by his own account he was still feeling pretty dicky. The mist was lifting in truth, and yellow spears of sunlight were thrusting themselves through like hat pins run through cloth.

"It'll be the better part of half an hour before the place's clear," he asserted, with one eye cocked at the sky and the other watching me.

"In the meanwhile we'd better go back to Miss Drummond and set her mind at rest," I suggested.

He trudged along at my elbow with a step that lacked its usual buoyancy, but the sidelong glances I stole at him every now and then showed me that he was fast recovering his spirits. The bruise on his forehead, seen now close at hand and in a better light, was not the fearsome thing I had at first taken it to be. True, it lent him an air of general disrepute, but then none of us were quite fit for the drawing-room. Even Moira, sheltered as she had been, showed very much the worse for wear. She greeted Cumshaw with a cheery smile, the bravest thing about her I thought, and a ready question as to his adventures. But he could tell her little more than that he had gone over the edge with us and rolled away until he brought up against the stone or whatever it was that had bruised his face so nicely. Our own story, what there was of it, was soon told, and a few glances about us showed that in the murk of the night and rain we had missed our footing and shot off the track a dozen feet or so to the level ground below. Above us waved the tall shapes of kingly gums, and below us lay vast spaces of bracken. Beyond that we could form little idea as to our position, though the mist was slowly drifting away now.

"The best thing to do, I suppose," I remarked, "is to get back to last night's camping-place and see what we can find of the stores. Of course we shouldn't have left them, but it's no use being wise after the event. We've to go back as quick as we can now, and maybe we can dig up something warm. That's supposing that everything isn't too wet to be used."

"As I remarked before, it's up to you," Cumshaw threw at me. "Lead on, Carstairs."

"If you can show me any way back to the main track, I'll lead on with pleasure," I told him. "There's none visible that I can see, and I don't fancy that my eyes are over dull."

Cumshaw said something under his breath, but before I could drop on him for it Moira interposed. "How about walking round at the foot of this ridge and seeing where it'll lead us to?" she suggested.

"That's as fine a plan as any," I answered. "We'll try it."

We did. We sauntered along listlessly for the best part of an hour, and then it struck me all of a sudden that we were rising rapidly.

"We're on the wrong track," I said, stopping short. "We didn't come down as steep a slope as this last night."

"You're right there, Carstairs. We didn't," Cumshaw said,

stopping short and looking about him with a puzzled air.

"Why not keep right on?" Moira advised. "It's just possible that we're working back to the track."

"We'll give it a chance," I said, after chewing the suggestion over in silence for a few minutes. "We'll keep on for ten minutes or so, and if it gets any worse we can always go back."

The ground became rougher at every step and finally in despair I called a halt. The sun was well up by this and the mist had cleared away from the hills, though filmy vapors still lingered in what I knew must be the hollows. In front was a causeway, strewn with boulders, and beyond that what I took to be a sea of wattles. I could see no use in progressing further in that direction, and I said so as succinctly as I could. Cumshaw was inclined to argue, but the consensus of opinion was against him. The outcome of it was that we decided to retrace our steps. Before we did so I suggested looking about for something that would give us an indication of our present position.

I stumbled on it quite by accident. Another step further and I would have fallen down the funnel-shaped opening that gaped at my feet. I drew back just in time to save myself, and for the second time that morning my heart gave a jump. To think that we had gone so close to missing it altogether! The thing, so to speak, had lain at our feet all the time. I turned about and searched the landscape for my companions. Moira was visible in the near distance; the wattles had swallowed Cumshaw.

"Cumshaw, Moira, I've found it!" I called at the top of my voice.

Moira whipped round at the sound of my voice. I waved to her and she came running towards me. A second later I saw Cumshaw come out of the shadows, and I yelled at him with all the power of my lungs. I don't know what he must have thought of the yelling, dancing, frantically waving figure that caught his eye. He must have fancied for a moment that I had gone mad. Then, in a flash, so he says, the truth dawned on him, and he in his turn sprinted towards me, the one idea uppermost in his mind being that the valley must have been found. At the same instant my soul was singing "Eureka!" and Moira was weeping and laughing at the same time.

"Cumshaw," I cried, as he came within speaking distance, "if that's not the funnel that your father and Bradby left the valley by you can call me a goggle-eyed Chinaman."

And then somehow we all seemed to be talking together.

"That must be the valley down under the wattles."

"I knew we'd find it."

"It only shows that one should never give in."

"If we hadn't fallen down that slope last night...."

"If I hadn't kept going when you all wanted to turn back, you mean."

"It's found now and that's the best part of it."

I must confess that I lost my head just as the others did. I should have known better, I suppose, than to go yelling out our discovery at the top of my lungs, but knowing's one thing and doing's altogether different. I've seen miners on the Lakekamu shouting themselves hoarse over even less of a discovery, seasoned men who knew how and when to hold their tongues. Could tyros like ourselves be blamed for what we did? I don't think so.

"That's the funnel right enough," Cumshaw said. "There can't possibly be two of the same kind in the same district. I'm sure this is the one; it's been described too often to me for there to be any mistake about it. But what's puzzling me is the valley.

There doesn't seem to be much of one here. All I can see is wattles, wattles whichever way I look."

"There's one way to settle it," I said in an aside to him, and I looked at Moira.

He gathered from my warning glance that I had something to say I didn't want her to hear, so he shifted out of earshot with me.

"There's things you don't want a girl to see," I explained as we walked off; "but if this is the valley the skeletons of those two horses should be down there somewhere," and I pointed over the edge of the funnel.

"I'll go down," he said with alacrity. "I guess it's my go. It's time I took some sort of a risk."

"You surely don't expect there'll be anything wrong?" I queried.

"I can't say," he answered with a shrug of his shoulders. "Anyway, I think you'd better get back to Miss Drummond. She's looking over this way, and in a minute or so she'll be asking awkward questions, if you don't go and tell her something."

"All right," I agreed. "Look as slippy as you can, but be careful. An injured man is always more or less of a nuisance, you know."

He grinned cheerfully at that, and then, without another word, turned on his heel and made off towards the funnel. I walked back to Moira.

"What are you going to do now?" she asked me suspiciously. "What's Mr. Cumshaw after?"

"He's going down through that funnel-shaped thing," I

answered. "He wants to see what's at the end of it."

The golden-brown eyes regarded me thoughtfully for a space and then: "Why didn't you go yourself instead of sending him?" she asked.

"It was his suggestion," I said defensively. "He seemed to think he had a better right than anyone else, so I didn't argue with him about it. I let him go."

"We could all have gone," she hinted.

"We could have," I agreed, "but we didn't."

In the meantime Cumshaw had lowered himself carefully down into the opening, felt about a bit with his feet, found a foothold, and then swung easily down from projecting ledge to projecting ledge. He emerged quite unexpectedly into a tangled mass of wattle. That puzzled him much, as it had puzzled me a few minutes previously; the elder Cumshaw's tale contained no mention of wattle save the golden barrier at the further side of the valley. Yet here was wattle as far as the eye could reach. It looked as if a generous scientist, like the man in H. G. Wells' "Food of the Gods," had let loose some power capable of forcing on this abnormal growth. The valley itself was in an undulating sea of vegetation. Had it been early in September the place would have been a vast expanse of golden glory, but as it was late March the dominant color note was that of grey-green. Under the circumstances it was as clear as daylight how the elder man had missed the place. It was buried under the rank growth, and all definable features, as we learnt later - everything that could be used as a leading mark - had disappeared or been swamped by the wattles. The bushes were not so thick about the lower entrance to the funnel as to impede Cumshaw's movements, and so he began to look about him in the hope of locating the one thing that would definitely identify the place. The horses had been shot close to the wall of rock, and it was a practical certainty that some trace of their bodies would be found in the vicinity. Ten minutes' close search brought to light a pile of bones that might or might not be those of the missing animals - Cumshaw had no knowledge of anatomical structure and so did not feel quite clear on that point - but the remarkable feature about them in his eyes was that they were all more or less blackened, and amongst them he found a heap of lime-dust, which he took to be bones reduced to their elemental form by the application of great heat. Still he felt justified in regarding the identity of the place as being sufficiently established, and without wasting any more time he returned the way he had come.

"There's no doubt about it," I agreed when I heard his tale. "This is the valley right enough. I vote on going down there at once. The old hut can't be far away, and it'll be somewhere for us to camp in and fix up our clothes. And that reminds me that one of us'll have to go back for our stores and extra clothes. There's no need for both of us to go; one will do. However that can wait until we find the hut."

"I'm not hungry," Moira said, "and I think my clothes are practically dry. The sun's coming out now, and I don't see why we should feel any the worse for last night's adventures if we only take reasonable care of ourselves."

"If that's the case," I remarked, "let us go down by all means."

I sent Cumshaw down first, as he was the only one of us who was familiar with the place, and then I handed Moira down to him. Or, rather, I helped her down; Moira at the best of times is no light weight. For a moment we stood blinking at the entrance to the funnel, and then Moira caught my arm in her impulsive way and cried, "Come on, Jim! Let's enter into Paradise!"

I smiled at her quaintness and made to follow her, but Cumshaw interposed quickly. "Not that way," he said. "This is the way." He glanced at me as he spoke, and I realised that he was taking us by a path that would lead us away from the mouldering bones.

The ground was rough underfoot, and the matted cover of vegetation that effectually hid stray boulders from view made it all the worse. In places the wattle grew over our heads in a profusion that was almost tropical, and more than once we would have lost our way had I not taken our bearings at the start, and thus was able to guide the party by means of my pocket-compass.

"In your father's day there was a wood hereabouts," I said to Cumshaw presently. "There doesn't seem to be one now."

"There doesn't," he said. "Can you understand how practically the entire physical features of the place have changed so much?"

"Frankly I can't. But they apparently have, and that's about all we can say. We'll just have to keep our eyes open and trust to luck."

"Our luck seems to have held good so far," Moira said, turning to me with high hope in her face.

"Mind your footing," I said warningly. "You want to watch every inch of the way. There's all sorts of rocks and boulders under this stuff."

"I'll be careful," she smiled, and scarcely were the words out of her mouth than her foot caught in something. She pitched forward on her face before I could spring to her assistance. I lifted her up carefully, but she seemed none the worse for her fall.

"I don't know what it was that tripped me," she confided. "It wasn't a boulder or anything of the sort. I think it was a log of wood, yet my foot seemed to catch underneath it."

I was on the point of offering a suggestion, but something held me silent, and instead I dropped down on my knees and felt feverishly in the undergrowth. Of course it was a silly thing to do - there might have been snakes and all manner of noxious crawling things there - but I didn't think of that at the time. I was too intent on solving the riddle. My hand touched something.... I straightened up and faced the others.

"Moira and Cumshaw," I said. "I've found the hut. That's a piece of it there." Bending down, I dragged to light a rough-hewn beam that possibly had been the threshold plank. It was weather-worn, and in places the fungus had grown thickly on it; but I could see for all that that it had been warped and twisted and charred in the blaze of a fire. Three pairs of eyes met across the plank, and three lips put the same idea into words.

"There's been a fire here," we said in chorus.

"And that," I added on my own account, for the benefit of the others who had not jumped to the same conclusion as I had, "and that explains everything that's puzzled us since we entered the valley. There's been a bush fire here at some period during the last twenty years. It destroyed the hut, it burnt down the wood, and it made that pile of lime you found, Cumshaw."

"What pile was that?" Moira queried quickly. "I didn't see any."

"Mr. Cumshaw passed a pile in the bushes as we came along," I said off-handedly. "The heat must have rendered the stones down."

She accepted my explanation at its face value.

"No wonder the place remained hidden," I ran on. "If you'll look over east, where there should be a lone tree, you won't find any. It's wattle everywhere you look. The fire cleared out all the trees and forced the wattle on in their place. If you came by here on any side but the one we came by you'd take this to be just an ordinary hollow full of wattle."

"You're talking nothing else but wattle," Cumshaw interrupted. "What has the wattle to do with the fire anyway?"

"Why, don't you see?" I cried. "Without the fire there wouldn't have been any wattle here. The seed'll lie dormant in the ground for years sometimes; it takes great heat to germinate them. That's why wattle always springs up in profusion after there's been a bush fire. The same thing happens with grass, the coarser kinds, though to a lesser extent."

"I see," he said gravely. "It means that we are back just where we began."

"It doesn't mean anything of the sort," I said quickly. "All this is in our favor. We're better off than we were before."

"I don't see how that is," he replied.

"But it is," I persisted, "and I'll show you why when the time comes. And now there's plenty to be done. One of us has to go back for the provisions that we left behind last night, and the other's got to stop here with Miss Drummond and run up a bit of a bark humpy that'll keep off the wind and won't let the rain through. Now if you're as hungry as I am you'll understand just how pressing the need of that food is. It's you or I, Cumshaw. Which of us is to go?"

"I'll toss you," Cumshaw offered.

I nodded, and he drew a coin from out his pocket and spun it in the air.

"Heads!" I called.

We bent down over it. "It's tail," said Cumshaw. "I go back for the food," I said.

I straightened up and spoke seriously to the pair of them. "Cumshaw," I said, "do as much as you can while I'm away, and keep one eye on the horizon all the time. You must remember that there's always danger about; the luck's been with us so far, but it may turn any minute, and our rivals are just the sort of men who'd come on you suddenly and shoot before you could say 'Jack Robinson.' And as for you, Moira, keep out of harm's way and do what you can towards keeping a good lookout. I'm going across to the other side, as I reckon that we must have travelled round the valley last night."

"You'll be careful, won't you, Jim, dear?" Moira whispered.

"Aren't I always careful?" I said. "It's you that's got to watch out. Now, one kiss, dear. I'll be back as soon as I can possibly manage it."

* * * * *

Five minutes later I had gained the further wall of the valley, and found that, with the help of the bushes, it was the easiest thing imaginable for an active man like myself to haul himself up over the ridge and drop on the track which Abel Cumshaw and the late Mr. Bradby had trodden so many years before. I took my bearings carefully, then snapped up my pocket-compass and set off down the road with as jaunty a swing as I was capable of. I had long got over my stiffness, and now that the sun was shining brightly I began to feel more confident than ever that all was going well. If it had not been for the terrible way in which the dread purpose of our rivals had been brought home to us already I would have felt absolutely at ease. As it was I did not let my rosy anticipations of the future interfere at all with my sense of caution.

CHAPTER V

DIES IRAE

As a matter of strict fact the place was much further away than I had anticipated. We must have wandered a considerable distance in the confusion of the evening's storm and covered more ground than we had thought. I had positioned the sun as I had left the valley and judged the time to be about eleven o'clock; "that," I thought, "will bring me back by two at the very latest." But really it was close on five, and the shadows were already dropping down over the country-side before I was ready to return. I found our little store of goods intact, though most of them were rain-soaked, and as a measure of good fortune I retrieved the tent whose sudden departure had been the primary cause of our hurriedly shifting camp. There was a fair load in all, but when I had made it up and rolled everything packwise in the tent and fastened it on my shoulders with what odd bits of string I found handy, there wasn't anything in it that would seriously try the strength of a seasoned explorer like myself. Then, because the night was beginning to draw in and I did not want to go stumbling through the valley in the dark, I set off at my top pace. I don't claim to be anything wonderful as far as walking is concerned, but if I were ever asked what I considered my record I would point back to that very night. I forced myself along, my whole being intent on reaching the valley before the sun slipped down behind the hills. I think it was more will-power than sheer physical strength that kept me moving. I was just a little anxious about Moira too. Cumshaw was a fine chap and clever in his own way, though he did have occasional spurts of temper; but he lacked my woodcraft experience, and I wasn't sure but what he might go to pieces if any prowlers pounced down on him unawares. Neither he nor Moira had ever come up against anything that would teach them to act as quickly as they could think, and, though they might work like niggers when they were under someone else's orders, an emergency that threw them on their own resources might find them seriously wanting.

The shadows lengthened as I sped along, the tired yellow sun slipped down behind the hills like a penny-into-the-slot machine, and the early April twilight touched all inanimate objects with its own drab lack of coloring. I had no fear of losing my way in the darkness - I had too much locality sense for that - but the possibilities of my being ambushed appeared too many to be pleasant. A hurrying man, who is also heavily-laden, cannot pick his footsteps with the meticulous care that he would like, and it seemed within the bounds of probability that some strange listener might start out on my track and put an abrupt period to my career of usefulness. I have an unqualified and not unreasonable objection to being cut off in what is practically the flower of my youth. I was afraid. I admit that quite frankly, and I have yet to find the man who has not known fear whenever he drifted into a tight corner. But fear is not the hall-mark of a coward; it is at worst a natural impulse to seek safety and take precautions, and at its best it is the intellectual penalty that a strong man pays for having a will-power that will not permit him to scurry away from danger and earth himself like a rabbit in its burrow.

I reached the valley without incident, scrambled down the historic slope, now as slippery as a child's mud-slide, and was half-way across the open space before I received my first shock. Some queer sixth sense pulled me up in mid-stride. I had heard nothing, I had seen nothing; but for all that I knew that a strange and obtrusive presence was very close to me. The New Guinea native can at times tell the presence of an enemy simply by his sense of smell, and I suppose I've lived so long amongst them that I have acquired something of this kind. Be this as it may, I was aware of the other man's proximity long before my faculties went into action and confirmed me in my belief.

I slipped my shoulders out of the pack-strings and dropped it noiselessly on the ground. At that precise instant I heard a stealthy movement on my left hand. It was so dark that I could not see an inch in front of my face, but a little eddy of the breeze brought me the merest whiff of stale tobacco - the sort of smell that comes from a pipe that has been put out before it has completely burnt away. It was that dead scent that always seems to hang about the vicinity of a newly quenched fire. I was so close that I caught the sound of the man's breathing. With every second breath there came a barely perceptible wheeze, and in an instant my mind flashed back to the night of the burglary in Bryce's house and the man I had caught coming out of the library. I was so sure of it that I wasted no further time in stalking him; no two men in the world could have that same regular wheezing breath. It requires a neat sense of distance to catch an invisible man round the throat when he and everything else tangible and real is hidden under cover of Stygian darkness; but this time I made the snatch of my life, and as luck would have it, had him by the windpipe before he realised that there was anyone within a quarter of a mile of him. I didn't give him a chance to cry out - I had no idea how close his friends were, if he had any - but just threw all my weight into my clutching hands and quietly but inexorably choked the life out of him. In the struggle his hat fell off and I released one hand and ran it through his hair. Up till then there was a lingering suspicion at the back of my mind, that after all I might have throttled Cumshaw by mistake, but the feel of that straight hair completely burked the last of my doubts. There was no possible chance of mistaking Cumshaw's curly crop for the strands I held in my free hand, for he suddenly went limp under my hands, and when I fumbled for his heart I could not feel it beating. At the time I felt rather cut up, and considered that I had practically killed the man in cold blood; but afterwards, when I came to reckon up the tally of disaster, I was sorry that I had passed him out so peacefully. There were a lot of other methods I might have used had I known in time. But then I didn't, and that makes all the difference.

Satisfied in my own mind that the stranger was out of action for good and all, I rose to my feet and threaded my way back to where I had left my pack. I slipped the strings over my shoulders and set off again in the direction I hoped to find Moira and my companion. But scarcely had I taken a dozen steps forward when the silence of the night was shattered by the report of a revolver, and in an instant a perfect fusillade had begun. I dropped all caution at that. Throwing the pack from off my shoulders, I drew my revolver as I ran. I simply tore across the intervening space like a red god of vengeance suddenly descended on a planet of sin. The sound of the shots had maddened me beyond all belief, and in my then mood I would have walked single-handed into a whole army. Luckily for myself I had not gone far before I collided with a wattle bush, and the scratches I received brought me back to a saner frame of mind. I saw with an appalling clarity of vision that I was taking the worst possible course. Cumshaw and Moira were being attacked - that was beyond question - and my game was to come upon the attackers unawares and either rout or put as many of them out of action as I could with the weapons at my command.

So when I moved off again I had slackened my pace down to a stealthy cat-like tread that took me along with an incredible absence of noise. As I moved forward I began to turn the configuration of the place over in my mind and wonder to what practical use I could put the fine natural cover of the bushes. As I could see none I put the matter out of my head and devoted all my energies to coming to immediate grips with the men who had murdered the eternal peace of the valley.

Presently I caught sight of a little red flash from one of the revolvers, but as I had no idea as to whose it was I held my hand and commenced to circle round the fight. It must be remembered, in order to gauge the seriousness of the situation, that the night was as black as the ace of spades, and that the only guide I had was the occasional flash from a revolver - a flash that might have come from either friend or foe; I had nothing to tell me which. It was in this queer fashion that I was progressing when the toe of my boot touched something soft and alien. I slipped down by the side of it and ran my hand over it. It was a man's body - the still warm body from which the pulsing life had suddenly been hurled. With my experience of the other man I had handled earlier in the night I felt for the hair, and, to my utter horror, I clutched a crop of short, crisp curls. It was Albert Cumshaw beyond a doubt. I did not waste a moment in useless sentimentality over the dead. The truth flashed across my mind with the blinding clearness of lightning. Moira was by herself, fighting like some heroic goddess against those other bestial savages. I know it is the fashion to picture men in such moments as going berserker, but I don't think in my case that I have ever been so sanely clear-headed in my life. It was a monstrous and incredible thing that this quiet little corner of the quietest little State in Australia should be polluted by the presence of the incarnate fiends that had murdered Bryce, that had killed Cumshaw, and were even now seeking to send Moira to join them in the shades. A cold, pitiless anger took possession of me, and I set about my work of vengeance as calmly as if I were going rabbit-shooting. I knew now of a surety that I could shoot at any man who came within range without fear or favor.

It was then I blessed my stars for the matted undergrowth and the wild profusion of wattle. The one deadened the sound of my movements and the other gave me all the cover I needed. The game was now fairly in my hands, and if I lost it would be through no one's fault but my own. It was quite evident on the face of it that the attacking force had no idea that a third party was maneuvering outside the range of fire, and I counted on that fact to assist me in my work. The one drawback at present was that I had no notion which was friend and which was foe. The shots seemed to come from all round the compass, and any one of them might be Moira's. It was quite on the cards that she was moving round in a circle, in the full knowledge that every time she fired she shot at an enemy, and again it was just as likely that she knew nothing at all about Cumshaw's death. Clearly it was a situation that called for an immense amount of care on my part.

I had no time to waste puzzling the matter out; whatever I did had to be done as quickly as possible, for I had no guarantee that the one-sided warfare might not terminate fatally at any moment. One of the attackers was just as likely to hit Moira as she was to hit him. I had slipped up the catch of my revolver long before this, and was carrying it in such a fashion that it could be fired instantly. I felt ready for any emergency, and the contingency that presently arose found me well prepared. There was a stealthy rush through the undergrowth, and a man backed hastily in my direction. I couldn't see him, but I knew that it was a man by the sound of the footsteps. There is always a perceptible difference between the footsteps of a man and a woman, but it requires a trained ear to pick it out. I slipped down into cover as he rushed back, and, judging more by sound than sight, I fired as he passed me. He came down heavily amidst a crash of breaking branches and the smashing of twigs. "I seem to be the only sure-footed man about to-night," I thought as the fellow thudded to the ground. At that precise moment, as if to give the lie direct to me, a deafening report sounded right in my ear, a pain as of a red-hot needle stabbed through my right shoulder, and I pitched forward on my face. Even as my nose ploughed through the soft soil it occurred to me to wonder if I had received a shot intended for the other man, or if he was not as dead as I had fancied and signalised his escape by shooting me in his turn. I was more scared than hurt, and I quickly picked myself up and clapped an anxious hand to my throbbing shoulder. The ball, by the feel of it, had done nothing worse than skim through the fleshy part of my arm, and I was in no wise incapacitated. I thanked my lucky stars that I was whole and entire, save for a spoonful or so of unwanted blood, for I rather guessed that I had heavy work ahead of me before I went to sleep that night.

Just as my mind was clearing again I became aware that someone was striking matches. I distinctly heard the scrape of one along the top of the box, and I fancied I saw a tiny phosphorescent glow such as a match makes when it misfires, but in that I may have been mistaken. As I watched for another flash it dawned on me that the artillery had ceased fire, and, for aught I knew to the contrary, I was probably the last bird topped off that night. Therefore the person with the matches could only be one of the victorious side, and was just as obviously counting up the casualties.

There came another little interlude of scraping, a match spluttered undecidedly for a moment and then glowed brightly. After the Stygian darkness the light came as a queer physical shock, and for the space of a heart-beat I blinked like an owl in broad daylight. I think the other person must have been just as much dazzled as I was, for the light died out and the glowing tip of the match fell to the ground without a movement from either of us. But it was followed almost instantly by another match, less damp than its fellow, for it splashed into light right away. And there in the little circle of radiance I caught sight of the one face on earth that I ever wished to see again.

"Moira!" I gasped and glided to her side.

She dropped the match in the surprise of the moment, and I heard her breath come and go before she answered, "You, Jim! Oh, I'm so glad! I thought perhaps...."

"They didn't," I said grimly, cutting across her thoughts. "It was the other way about."

"Mr. Cumshaw, Jim? Have you seen him anywhere?"

"No," I said truthfully enough. I hadn't seen him; it had been too dark, and I dared not strike a match.

"Oh, I'm afraid he's been shot. We got separated in the

darkness, and I don't know what happened to him."

"How did you get separated?" I queried quickly.

"We were making for the cave and I lost him in the dark. After that they started firing, and I just fired back, more to keep up my courage than anything."

"But where on earth did you get the revolver? You hadn't one of your own."

"Yes, I had, Jim. I brought it with me, and I didn't say anything because I thought you might laugh or else be angry with me."

"You've certainly shown that you know how to use it," I said dryly.

Something in my voice must have told her what had happened. "What do you mean?" she asked in a frightened tone. "Did I shoot anyone?"

"Yes," I said slowly. "You pinked me. Right in the shoulder. It's only a flesh-wound; nothing to worry about."

"I've hurt you and I didn't mean to," she wailed.

I reached out and seized her by the shoulders. "Look here, Moira," I said with a semblance of sternness in my voice, "you've done a man's work to-night and it's making you hysterical. Don't let it. Pull yourself together, for heaven's sake if not for mine."

I think it was just that last bit that brought her round. "I'm sorry, Jim," she said, though what there was to be sorry about was more than I could say.

"And now, Moira," I ran on before she had time to say anything more, "the sooner we finish that interrupted journey to the cave the better. It's not as good as the hut would be if it was still standing, but it gives us shelter, and that's the main thing. Also we can light a fire and sleep the night in peace, now that the gang seems to have been rubbed out for good."

She made no answer, so I took her arm, and thus we commenced our walk across the valley. I found the pack without any trouble, though my heart was in my mouth for fear that we would trip over poor Cumshaw's body. But the luck was with me that night, though it hadn't been with him, and I reached the pack and hoisted it on my shoulders without either of us striking any of the victims of the fight. The sting of the wound in my shoulder made the pack an uncomfortable burden, but I bore it as best I could, for I was afraid that Moira would notice me if I kept wriggling it into an easier position. So I fought the pain all the way to the cave, which we reached in something under five minutes. Moira did not speak a word all the way, and somehow I hadn't the heart to break the news of Cumshaw's death to her. It had to be done sooner or later, I knew, but I was inclined to put it off as long as possible.

Once in the cave I built a little fire of chips and dry bracken that had somehow escaped the rain. That done I turned with a clear conscience to the task of making tea. Moira, however, had forestalled me; the billy was already full, and she but awaited me to adjust the tripod of sticks that held it in its place over the fire. It was while I was bending over doing this that she must have noticed the bloodstains on my sleeve. At any rate, when I straightened up, she looked at me with accusation in her eyes.

"Why didn't you tell me before that it was as bad as that?" she asked.

"Because it isn't," I answered with cheerful paradox. But she would have none of my jesting, and if I hadn't allowed her to wash and bind it up right away I'm afraid I wouldn't have got any tea that night. When she finished she placed her hands upon my shoulders and kissed me full on the lips.

"My dear," she said brokenly, "you would die for me, I know, and yet I so little deserve your love."

I had tact enough to suppress the banality that was trembling on my lips.

* * * * *

"I wonder what could have happened to Mr. Cumshaw?" she remarked about an hour later. "You'd have thought he'd have been here long ago if he was all right."

"Maybe," I said, bending my head over the fire so she would not see my tell-tale face, "maybe he's not satisfied that this is our party."

There was an interval of silence and, though I did not look up, I knew that she was regarding me steadfastly. I could feel her eyes boring into my head like twin gimlets.

"Jim," she said suddenly and sharply, "what are you hiding from me? What has happened to Mr. Cumshaw? I know something has gone wrong by the way you're acting."

I raised my eyes to meet hers; it was impossible to hide it any longer. "The very worst that could happen," I said frozenly, and I dropped my head once more.

When I looked up again she was crying very softly to herself. I could understand her sorrow, and for once her regard for the man caused me no stab of pain; one cannot be jealous of the dead.

CHAPTER VI

THE SOLUTION

The grey light of the early dawn found me wide awake and alert. I felt much fatigued after my exertions of the previous night, and would dearly have liked to have slept an hour or so longer, but there was that to be done which would admit of no delay. Further out in the Valley lay three dead men, and I felt I must get them out of sight before Moira awoke. Accordingly I scribbled a short note of explanation on a leaf torn from my pocket-book, placed it in a conspicuous position, and, taking with me the light spade we had brought with us, I slipped noiselessly out of the cave. I found the bodies of our two enemies without any trouble, but, to my great surprise, there was no trace of Cumshaw. He had disappeared as utterly as if the earth had opened up and swallowed him. True, there were broken branches and snapped twigs galore, but of signs that would show me where the body had been taken or what had happened after I had left, there was absolutely none. For the moment I wondered if it had all been but a vivid dream, but the sight of the torn and scarred ground and the memory of the other two bodies told me that it was only too real. Obviously then the corpse had been moved, but where or by whom I could not say.

I spent the next half-hour in scouring the valley from end to end, yet when I had finished I was compelled to admit that I was no nearer to a solution than before. All the time, of course, there was a perfectly simple explanation staring me in the face, but it was so infernally obvious that I missed it.

As my search had not led me any further forward, I shut the matter out of my mind for the present and turned to the less engrossing though certainly more pressing task of burying the bodies that remained. The spot I chose for the grave seemed rather familiar to me, but for the moment I could not say just what it brought to my mind. I pegged away with the spade, and had already dug a fair-sized hole when, unexpectedly, the further side of the grave caved in. I swore under my breath at this brilliant result of my efforts, and, with the intention of clearing away the rubble, thrust my spade deep into the loose earth. It met with a solid obstruction, something that seemed to me like the root of a tree, or - At that I stopped dead. Could it be possible that I had struck the foundation of the hut?

The morning we entered the valley Moira had tripped over one of the loose logs that had once been part of the building, and at the time I had attached peculiar significance to the discovery; but now it appeared that I had actually gone one better. Without more ado I made the dirt fly, and in less time than it takes to tell I had shot away the covering earth and brought to light the object that had at first drawn my attention. I saw then, with a gasp of relief, that it was indeed the eastern foundation of the hut that I had unearthed. Whoever had built the place had built well, for the thick cross-piece still remained tightly nailed to the stout posts that had supported the foundation. The fire that had swept the neighbourhood had somehow failed to consume it, though subsequent developments had buried it under piles of bracken and dead brushwood. It was an amazing discovery, and under the circumstances the luckiest one imaginable. At the very least it enabled me to place one of the fixed points that were vital to the discovery of the plunder. At the same time it showed me how I might be able, with a little extra luck, to locate the sight of the burnt tree.

I went on with my digging.

Half an hour later I finished my self-imposed task, swung the spade over my shoulder, and prepared to return to the cave. I could see Moira in the distance moving towards me, and I guessed that my prolonged absence had made her feel somewhat uneasy.

"Where have you been all the time, Jim?" was her greeting. "I was just beginning to fear that something had happened to you."

"Something has," I answered, "but not in the way you mean. I've located the exact position of the hut. That piece of wood you tripped over must have been only a log that escaped being fully consumed. We're well on the way towards finding the treasure now."

She eyed me keenly before she spoke again, and I knew what she was going to ask me almost before she put her thoughts into words.

"Was that all you went to do?" she asked.

"No," I said, "I came out mainly to bury the dead."

She gave a little shudder at that, but her voice was steady enough as she said, "And you did? All of them?"

I shook my head. "Not him," I said ungrammatically.

"Why?" she demanded, with Heaven knows what idea at the back of the question.

"Because," I said distinctly, "because he wasn't there."

"Jim, whatever do you mean?" she cried.

"I can't say any more than I've just said," I told her. "When I went to look I found he wasn't where I'd left him last night, and, though I searched the valley from end to end, I couldn't find sign or sight of him."

"It's impossible," she asserted. "You can't make a dead man fade into thin air like that. If he's not in the valley, he's been taken out of it."

"And who's taken him out?" I countered. "There's only two ways out. Nobody's passed us during the night, and anyone that went out through the wattles would leave a trail like an elephant."

"That's true enough," she admitted crestfallenly. And then she turned on me swiftly. "Jim," she cried, "it's possible.... He might...."

The idea jumped into my mind at almost the same moment, but it seemed too preposterous for belief.

"No," I interrupted. "It isn't. He couldn't. Moira, I tell you he was as dead as a door-nail when I reached him."

She made a little gesture of despair as she realised to the full the bitter futility of attempting to solve the puzzle, yet I had a feeling that she had not quite given up hope. She did not make any further remark on the way back to the cave, and she certainly wasn't as much thrilled by my discovery of the ruins of the hut as I had expected her to be. I let her be; it's never safe to divert the current of a woman's thoughts.

I stepped into the cave ahead of her, and no sooner had I passed from the light outside into the interior darkness than a crisp voice snapped at me.

"Hands up!" it said tersely.

I shot my hands into the air more as a measure of precaution than anything else, for I recognised the voice - the voice that I thought had been silenced for ever.

"Cumshaw!" I ejaculated.

I could not see him since he was lurking right in the interior shadows, but some electric quality in the air convinced me that his astonishment was as great as mine. Nevertheless he answered me in tones that were as calm as could be.

"So it's yourself, Carstairs," he said. "I'll have to apologise for being a little previous with you, but you must remember that you are standing in your own light and I can only see your outline. And - Ah! here is Miss Drummond too."

He came towards us at that, a dark figure looming out of the gloom. And the next instant we had him one by each hand and pelted him with questions.

"I thought you were dead," I said. "How did you come alive again?"

"What happened?" Moira asked.

"How did you get here and what were you doing all night?"

"One question at a time," he said laughingly. "It seems pretty obvious that I'm not dead, doesn't it?"

"It does," I admitted. "But you were dead, or you appeared to be, when I left you last night."

"I don't quite understand," he said. "What do you mean?"

I told him then how I had stumbled across his body on my return the previous evening, how I had identified him, and, satisfied that he was dead, had left him to attend to more pressing business. I related how I had scoured the valley that very morning and failed to find the least trace of him. What was the explanation of the seeming miracle? I asked.

"There's nothing miraculous about it," he said. "Last night I must have been creased, sort of stunned, you know. The bullet didn't go near any vital part. It just ploughed along the back of my neck and knocked me unconscious. I suppose I would seem pretty dead to anyone who stumbled across me. It's not always so easy for a layman to tell whether a man is really dead or not. However, I remember coming-to just on daylight, and hearing someone crashing through the bushes. It struck me then that I didn't know how things had panned out, so I'd better take cover until I made sure. So when you were hunting for me I was running away from you, keeping a couple of jumps ahead all the time. I gradually edged round towards the cave, and was just in time to see a dim figure slip out into the bushes. I wasn't close enough to see more clearly. Miss Drummond, you say. Yes, I suppose so; but I didn't know that then. However, as the cave seemed deserted after that I took possession with the intention of turning the tables. And then - But you know the rest yourself. How much further have we got?"

"Lots," I said. "The others are dead and buried, and I have found the original site of the hut. Once we locate the lone tree we're right."

"That should be easy enough," said Moira with a woman's airy assurance.

Cumshaw watched us both with a queer smile flickering about his lips.

"What do you think of it, Carstairs?" he said at length.

"I don't fancy there'll be much difficulty in that," I answered. "It should be plain sailing from now onwards."

"It strikes me," he said, "that we're just entering upon the toughest stretch of the lot. However, the sooner we get to work the better. I vote we start right away."

"But, Mr. Cumshaw," Moira protested, "do you think you feel

well enough?"

"Miss Drummond," he answered, "I've got pains all down my neck, and my head's humming like a hive of bees, and I've got incipient rheumatics in every joint in my body from lying all night on the damp ground. It's bad enough to have all that wrong with me, without being compelled to spend another day in idleness. No, if I get to work at once I'll feel much better. Work, you know, is a good soporific."

"I suppose you know best," she conceded, a little doubtfully.

"I've been thinking things over," I remarked as we made our way back to the site of the hut, "and it's just struck me that something I once heard Bryce say might have some bearing on the matter. The night those chaps burgled us he said, 'They're up a gum-tree when they should be under one.' I'm not so sure of the exact words now, but that's the substance of them anyway."

"But," Cumshaw objected, "he didn't know as much about the Valley then as we do now."

"Quite so," I said. "I never thought he really meant anything by what he said, but that remark's been running through my head. It seems to me that everyone right through has been obsessed by the idea of the tree, and now that it's disappeared we're at a loose end. Everybody, from your father and Bradby down to Bryce and ourselves, has taken it for granted that a tree's vital to the solution."

"Isn't it?" Cumshaw queried quickly.

I shook my head. "Not in the least," I said. "If the tree was absolutely necessary it'd mean that we'd have to wait until 3rd or 4th of December, the day on which Bradby buried the treasure, and the only day of the year on which the sun, the tree and the threshold of the hut would be in an exact line. Bryce's idea of having to wait three months must have been conceived in the belief that the 3rd or 4th June would answer equally well. It might, but I'm not so sure about it. I guess there'd be a lot of difference in the declination of the sun. But now the tree's gone we're left without that seemingly necessary leading mark."

"What are we going to do about it?" Cumshaw demanded.

"We can't give up after having gone so far," said Moira.

"We're not," I told her. "There's a way out of it, and the simplest way on earth. It's so infernally simple that we've all overlooked it. It narrows down to a simple problem in geometry. Do you remember what the cypher said?"

"'When the Lone Tree, the hut door and the rising sun are in line measure seven feet east. Then face direct north, draw another line at right angles to the previous one, extending for twelve feet. Dig then.'" He rattled through the directions so rapidly that I knew he must have had them off by heart.

"That's it," I said, while the others listened in breathless interest. "Now this is the position to my mind: The line that runs through the doorway, the tree and the sun must go due east. The sun at that time of the year would be due east. Well, all we have to do is to cast our east line, carry it along for seven feet, and then turn so that we are facing direct north."

"And at right angles to the previous line," Moira reminded me.

"It's the same thing," I said. "Direct north runs at right angles to direct east, if you want to know. However, when we've got our north line we follow it for twelve feet, and after that we dig. Quite possibly Bradby made some slight variation - he wouldn't have the necessary instruments to make his figures absolutely exact - but, as I've said before, I don't see that we can go very far wrong. Whatever variation there is won't matter much once we start digging. If we allow a foot or so in all directions we'll be on the safe side. What do you think, Cumshaw?"

"Well," he said slowly, "it sounds feasible enough, and if it turns out as well in practice as it does in theory I'll have nothing to say against it."

"There's only one way of making sure," I said tentatively.

Moira turned on me. "What's that?" she asked with unfeigned interest.

"Trying and seeing for ourselves," I answered. "Here we are, right on the very spot, so why not put it to the test?"

Neither of them answered. A queer, speculative look crept into Moira's eyes and Cumshaw paled a little beneath his tan. It was the crucial moment of the expedition, and the mere adoption of my suggestion meant that in the next few minutes we would be face to face with either failure or success - none of us knew which. While we were in ignorance there was always room for hope, but the instant our investigation was concluded the matter would be settled for good or for evil.

"Well," I asked, "what about it?"

"I suppose we've got to do it some time," Cumshaw said slowly. "We might as well do it first as last. What do you say, Miss Drummond?"

"Ye-es," said Moira in a half-whisper. "Ye-es, I suppose we had better."

"And you, Carstairs?"

"Nothing venture, nothing win," I quoted gaily. "Anyway it's my suggestion, and I'm not going to fall down on it. I didn't bring the spade along just for the fun of carrying it."

"Go on then," Cumshaw said.

Then commenced the operation of locating the position of the treasure. As the one most used to such things I snapped open my pocket-compass, took a line from the mouldering ruin that had once been the threshold of the hut, and proceeded to calmly measure off the requisite distance. The others followed my movements with breathless interest; Cumshaw's cheeks were still pale, partly from the stress of emotion and partly, I fancy, because he feared that, even at the last, Fate would play a trick on us and bring the work of two generations to nothing. Two little red spots glowed in Moira's cheeks, and in her eyes was an opalescent glow that spoke of suppressed excitement. I wasn't so carried away by my feelings as the others were - I had been trained in a rough school, and my training had taught me at all times to keep an adequate control over my emotions - but the romance of the adventure and the excitement of the game had penetrated even my thick skin, and the mere fact that others hung breathlessly on my movements swayed me a little from the normal. That streak of vanity which is in all of us came to the surface, as it does with the best of men at the best of times.

I didn't see how I could possibly make a mistake, and the only thing that troubled me was the likelihood of some stray prospector having stumbled on the hoard by accident. At last I reached the spot where the north line ended, and then calmly and methodically I took off my coat, folded it, and laid it on the ground. I rolled up my shirt sleeves and seized the spade in my hands. The others watched me with apprehensive eyes.

CHAPTER VII

THE ADVENTURE CLOSES

I could hear Moira's quick breaths come and go as I worked, and with each shovelful of soil I turned Cumshaw craned his head a little further forward.

"Three foot, maybe three foot six," Cumshaw said once, in a voice that was curiously hoarse. The remark puzzled me for a moment, and then in a flash I recollected that his father had told Bryce that the hole where the gold was buried would be three feet or three feet six deep at a guess.

I went on digging. The hole deepened and widened, and still nothing appeared. I paused in my work and flung the damp perspiration from my forehead with a grimy hand. I had been working eagerly, excitedly.

"I'll take a hand now," Cumshaw offered with surprising alacrity.

I shook my head and stabbed the spade further into the earth. It struck something soft which yet offered a remarkable resistance to the progress of the instrument. And then in an instant I was down on my knees, the steaming sting of my perspiring face all forgotten in the wild intense eagerness of my discovery. I flung the spade about like a mad-man, and my breath came and went through my teeth with a hissing sound like that of escaping steam. I was mud and muck from head to foot and my hands were caked with clay, but that did not matter. Nothing mattered save the one startling fact that I had struck something that answered to the description of the stuff we were seeking. At last, after seemingly eternal hours of incredible toil, though in reality it couldn't have been more than a few seconds, the earth came away, and my spade lay bare four bags of mouldering leather - four torn and decaying things through which came the dull golden gleam of minted metal. With a smothered cry Cumshaw threw himself on the saddle-bags and hugged and clawed them like a man gone demented. For the moment there came a curious vulpine look into his face, and then it passed so swiftly that I could have fancied that it had never been there or anywhere else save in my imagination.

"We've found it at last," I said, and was surprised to find how thin my voice had become. It was the first rational word since I had begun to dig, and it acted on Cumshaw like a douche of cold water. He dropped the bags as if he had been stung, and climbed out of the hole rather shamefacedly.

Moira opened her mouth as if to speak and then shut it again. Ludicrous as it all looked, it was sufficient to show me just how unbalanced sane people can become at the sight of gold. The three of us looked at each other, and then I fancy we all laughed, albeit a little hysterically.

The rest is soon told. We got the rotting bags out somehow, and portion of their contents spilled out on the ground, though we didn't mind that at the time. There was more money in each of the bags than any one of us had ever handled before. In the light of what happened afterwards I'm positive that it was Cumshaw who suggested filling up the hole.

"A good idea," I thought. A gaping hole in the ground might attract the attention of strangers and lead to further enquiries - the kind of enquiries that would not be welcomed by us. I had thrown all but the last shovelful in when Cumshaw drew something from his pocket, looked at it a moment, and then, with a muttered exclamation, threw it into the hole and trod it deep into the earth. I got but the one look at it, and it seemed to me to be an ordinary leather-covered pocket-book. I was on the point of asking him the meaning of his action when I chanced to glance up at his face, and what I saw there made me shut my lips down like a steel trap. I said nothing, and beyond my first natural start of surprise I don't think I gave myself away at all.

* * * * *

It doesn't matter just how much we made out of it. If I were to write down the exact figures no one would believe them or me; but when I say that neither Cumshaw nor I - for Moira pooled her share with mine after all - will have to do a hand's turn again as long as we live, some idea can be gained of what was in those four decaying saddle-bags. To place gold, more especially minted coin, in circulation in this year of grace one thousand nine hundred and twenty requires more ingenuity than most men are possessed of, and frankly I could see no way out of it for many a long day. But in the end I struck an unexpected solution. What that solution was is neither here nor there: the expedients I resorted to would, if written down, fill a longer and perhaps a more exciting volume than this. Some day, when old age is creeping on me and the good opinion of my neighbours has almost ceased to matter, I may tell the tale in its entirety.

As we had no desire to attract more attention than we could help we did not attempt to take the gold along with us. Instead we buried it in a secluded spot not far from the railway, and a week or so later Cumshaw and I returned in the car for it.

* * * * *

"I wonder," I said, "how those chaps managed to find out so much about everything? Of course they were paralleling Bryce's investigations, but that doesn't explain all; they knew more about some things than he did himself."

We were sitting round the fire one evening a month or so later. Moira and I had just returned from our honeymoon, and Cumshaw had dropped in with the news that his father was in the hands of a noted alienist who hoped in time to completely cure the old man. The announcement had set us talking about our recent experiences, and *apropos* of them I had uttered the above remark.

"I've often wondered," Moira said, "how they first learnt about the treasure."

There was silence for a space and then Cumshaw spoke. "I rather fancy," he said, "that they knew about its existence long before Mr. Bryce did."

Moira shot a startled glance at him and I said, "Whatever do you mean?"

"You remember that pocket-book I threw into the trench the day we found the treasure?"

I nodded. "Yes," said Moira breathlessly.

"I found that in the grass early in the morning before I went up to the cave. It was a diary belonging to a man named Alick Blane. I didn't read it right through - I didn't have the time for one thing - but what I did see told me all I wanted to know. I buried it in the trench because I did not want what was written in the book to be published to the world. It was one of those things that are better kept out of sight and circulation."

"But what was it?" I queried.

He looked at us a moment as if debating with himself whether or not to tell us.

"Alick Blane's father was the trooper who shot Bradby," he said, and left us to imagine all the rest.

George Eliot
George Gissing
George MacDonald
George Meredith
George Orwell
George Sylvester Viereck
George Tucker
George W. Cable
George Wharton James
Gertrude Atherton
Gordon Casserly
Grace E. King
Grace Gallatin
Grace Greenwood
Grant Allen
Guillermo A. Sherwell
Gulielma Zollinger
Gustav Flaubert
H. A. Cody
H. B. Irving
H.C. Bailey
H. G. Wells
H. H. Munro
H. Irving Hancock
H. Rider Haggard
H. W. C. Davis
Haldeman Julius
Hall Caine
Hamilton Wright Mabie
Hans Christian Andersen
Harold Avery
Harold McGrath
Harriet Beecher Stowe
Harry Castlemon
Harry Coghill
Harry Houidini
Hayden Carruth
Helent Hunt Jackson
Helen Nicolay
Hendrik Conscience
Hendy David Thoreau
Henri Barbusse
Henrik Ibsen
Henry Adams
Henry Ford
Henry Frost
Henry James
Henry Jones Ford
Henry Seton Merriman
Henry W Longfellow
Herbert A. Giles
Herbert Carter
Herbert N. Casson
Herman Hesse
Hildegard G. Frey
Homer
Honore De Balzac
Horace B. Day
Horace Walpole
Horatio Alger Jr.
Howard Pyle
Howard R. Garis
Hugh Lofting
Hugh Walpole
Humphry Ward
Ian Maclaren
Inez Haynes Gillmore
Irving Bacheller
Isabel Hornibrook
Israel Abrahams
Ivan Turgenev
J.G.Austin
J. Henri Fabre
J. M. Barrie
J. Macdonald Oxley
J. S. Fletcher
J. S. Knowles
J. Storer Clouston
Jack London
Jacob Abbott
James Allen
James Andrews
James Baldwin
James Branch Cabell
James DeMille
James Joyce
James Lane Allen
James Lane Allen
James Oliver Curwood
James Oppenheim
James Otis
James R. Driscoll
Jane Austen
Jane L. Stewart
Janet Aldridge
Jens Peter Jacobsen
Jerome K. Jerome
John Burroughs
John Cournos
John F. Kennedy
John Gay
John Glasworthy
John Habberton
John Joy Bell
John Kendrick Bangs
John Milton
John Philip Sousa
Jonas Lauritz Idemil Lie
Jonathan Swift
Joseph A. Altsheler
Joseph Carey
Joseph Conrad
Joseph E. Badger Jr
Joseph Hergesheimer
Joseph Jacobs
Jules Vernes
Julian Hawthrone
Julie A Lippmann
Justin Huntly McCarthy
Kakuzo Okakura
Kenneth Grahame
Kenneth McGaffey
Kate Langley Bosher
Kate Langley Bosher
Katherine Cecil Thurston
Katherine Stokes
L. A. Abbot
L. T. Meade
L. Frank Baum
Latta Griswold
Laura Dent Crane
Laura Lee Hope
Laurence Housman
Lawrence Beasley
Leo Tolstoy
Leonid Andreyev
Lewis Carroll
Lewis Sperry Chafer
Lilian Bell
Lloyd Osbourne
Louis Hughes
Louis Tracy
Louisa May Alcott
Lucy Fitch Perkins
Lucy Maud Montgomery
Luther Benson
Lydia Miller Middleton
Lyndon Orr
M. Corvus
M. H. Adams
Margaret E. Sangster
Margret Howth
Margaret Vandercook

Margret Penrose
Maria Edgeworth
Maria Thompson Daviess
Mariano Azuela
Marion Polk Angellotti
Mark Overton
Mark Twain
Mary Austin
Mary Catherine Crowley
Mary Cole
Mary Hastings Bradley
Mary Roberts Rinehart
Mary Rowlandson
M. Wollstonecraft Shelley
Maud Lindsay
Max Beerbohm
Myra Kelly
Nathaniel Hawthrone
Nicolo Machiavelli
O. F. Walton
Oscar Wilde
Owen Johnson
P.G. Wodehouse
Paul and Mabel Thorne
Paul G. Tomlinson
Paul Severing
Percy Brebner
Peter B. Kyne
Plato
R. Derby Holmes
R. L. Stevenson
R. S. Ball
Rabindranath Tagore
Rahul Alvares
Ralph Bonehill
Ralph Henry Barbour
Ralph Victor
Ralph Waldo Emmerson
Rene Descartes
Rex Beach
Rex E. Beach
Richard Harding Davis
Richard Jefferies
Richard Le Gallienne
Robert Barr
Robert Frost
Robert Gordon Anderson
Robert L. Drake
Robert Lansing
Robert Lynd
Robert Michael Ballantyne
Robert W. Chambers
Rosa Nouchette Carey
Rudyard Kipling
Samuel B. Allison
Samuel Hopkins Adams
Sarah Bernhardt
Sarah C. Hallowell
Selma Lagerlof
Sherwood Anderson
Sigmund Freud
Standish O'Grady
Stanley Weyman
Stella Benson
Stella M. Francis
Stephen Crane
Stewart Edward White
Stijn Streuvels
Swami Abhedananda
Swami Parmananda
T. S. Ackland
T. S. Arthur
The Princess Der Ling
Thomas A. Janvier
Thomas A Kempis
Thomas Anderton
Thomas Bailey Aldrich
Thomas Bulfinch
Thomas De Quincey
Thomas Dixon
Thomas H. Huxley
Thomas Hardy
Thomas More
Thornton W. Burgess
U. S. Grant
Valentine Williams
Various Authors
Vaughan Kester
Victor Appleton
Victoria Cross
Virginia Woolf
Wadsworth Camp
Walter Camp
Walter Scott
Washington Irving
Wilbur Lawton
Wilkie Collins
Willa Cather
Willard F. Baker
William Dean Howells
William le Queux
W. Makepeace Thackeray
William W. Walter
William Shakespeare
Winston Churchill
Yei Theodora Ozaki
Yogi Ramacharaka
Young E. Allison
Zane Grey

www.ingramcontent.com/pod-product-compliance
Lightning Source LLC
LaVergne TN
LVHW090601110826
845146LV00001B/213